A REST IN THE COURT

A DRIVE TO THE MI...

del Coronado

A DIP IN THE SURF

...ado Beach Calif.

Hotel del Coronado
HISTORY

First printing February 2013.
Printed in Korea.

Published by
Hotel del Coronado Heritage Department
1500 Orange Avenue
Coronado, CA 92118
619.435.6611
www.hoteldel.com

Copies may be ordered from
Hotel del Coronado Retail Department
1500 Orange Avenue
Coronado, CA 92118
888.236.1357

Other books published by the Hotel del Coronado:
Celebrating Over a Century of Romance at the Hotel del Coronado:
   Engagements, Weddings, Honeymoons and Anniversaries, 2012
Wish You Were Here: Vintage Postcards from the
   Hotel del Coronado, 2010
Building the Dream: The Design and Construction of the
   Hotel del Coronado, 2008
"The Loveliest Hotel You Can Imagine": A Child's View of the
   Hotel del Coronado, 2005
Beautiful Stranger: The Ghost of Kate Morgan and the
   Hotel del Coronado, 2002

The Hotel del Coronado has made every effort to ensure
the accuracy of this text. If you have additional information
about the resort's history, please contact:

Heritage Department
Hotel del Coronado
1500 Orange Avenue
Coronado, CA 92118
619.435.6611
www.hoteldel.com

Contents

In the Beginning

It Started with a Dream

In the mid-1880s, Elisha Babcock, Jr., and Hampton Story, retired Midwestern businessmen, enjoyed boating over to the undeveloped peninsula of Coronado to hunt and fish. Newly settled in San Diego, these California transplants were captivated by Coronado's promise — an expansive stretch of pristine Pacific coast, right on San Diego Bay.

The city of San Diego offered its own promise — it was beginning to boom. With the potential for increased rail access, investors from around the country poured into the area, buying up property and building up businesses. Between November 1885 — when the first branch of the transcontinental railroad reached San Diego — and 1887, the population of the city reached an estimated 35,000 people, up from an estimated 5,000 in 1885.

With San Diego's bustling economy, along with a steady influx of new residents and visitors, Babcock and Story — lifelong entrepreneurs — decided it was the perfect time to develop Coronado into a resort community, complete with a grand seaside hotel, one that would become "the talk of the western world." The area's Southern California location would be a major draw for America's wealthy Victorians, thanks to its wonderful weather, exotic scenery and absence of many urban diseases.

In 1885, Babcock and Story (aided by a handful of investors) purchased the entire "island" of Coronado for $110,000, forming the Coronado Beach Company. Although Coronado is technically a peninsula — joined to the mainland of California by a thin spit of land called the Silver Strand — in the early days during high tide, Coronado became a true island.

Once the peninsula was purchased, development proceeded quickly: Transportation systems were established (wharves and ferries for carrying cargo and visitors); fresh water was piped in under San Diego Bay; an electrical plant was built; roads were laid out (a grid pattern for the center of town, more undulating roads along Coronado's graceful coastline); parkland was set aside; and trees were planted. Babcock and Story reserved the spectacular Pacific coastline for the soon-to-be-built Hotel del Coronado. Other business enterprises were kept to Orange Avenue, a meandering thoroughfare that extended from San Diego Bay (the arrival point via ferry for Coronado visitors) through the center of town, ending at the oceanfront site of the future hotel.

By 1886, the establishment of Coronado was well under way, and a land auction was held on November 13. This highly publicized event drew an estimated 6,000 people, and by the end of the first day, $1 million in lots had been sold. With these profits in hand, Babcock and Story began to plan and build the Hotel del Coronado, aided by Illinois architect James Reid.

Building the Dream ... and Furnishing It

In the 1880s, most of Southern California was undeveloped and unpopulated. Accordingly, nearly all materials and manpower required to build The Del were imported from outside the San Diego area, including wood and workers — mostly from Northern California and the Midwest. Other materials were manufactured on site, such as lumber (in a planing mill), bricks (in a kiln) and nails (metal shop and iron works); even early employees were imported. Below is a variety of construction, furnishing and staffing highlights, as reported by the *San Diego Union*.

11.18.86: *The plans for the great Coronado Hotel arrived last night.*

1.18.87: *Mrs. E.S. Babcock, Jr., wife of the President of the Coronado Beach Company, yesterday cast the first shovel of dirt for the excavation for the foundation.*

3.12.87: *[Lot] sales without parallel ... and the property has never moved so fast [a reported $600,000 in sales]. The whole property is now illuminated with electricity, making the night as bright as day.*

c. 6.87: *A large portion of the lathing is finished.*

c. 7.87: *Judge Puterbaugh toasted "the man with the brain to conceive and the nerve to execute great enterprises, E.S. Babcock, Jr." Mr. Babcock responded with a humorous reference to the impropriety of criminals speaking at public meetings.*

8.11.87: *Captain Nichols, of the American ship* Frank Pendleton, *has presented Mr. Babcock with an Australian tree fern from the Antipodes. It is a beautiful specimen, and will be placed in the large court ... an ornament as well as a curiosity.*

8.16.87: *At the brickyard, 50,000 bricks are turned out daily; some 40,000 are used at the hotel, and the remainder [are] put aside for [sale] ... in San Diego.*

Continued on page 10

8.19.87: *About five carloads of windows and door sashes and other joined materials are used at the hotel daily.*

8.23.87: *The number of shingles necessary for roofs and sides is 2,000,000.*

8.24.87: *The payroll for the week amounts to $8,802.*

10.7.87: *Mr. Babcock is said to be in favor of painting the hotel white.*

10.15.87: *Sightseers about the hotel become so numerous that the company has been compelled to put watchmen at the entrance.*

10.18.87: *Ten tons of iron has been used in the construction of the hotel.*

11.5.87: *The draftsmen in [architect] Mr. Reid's office are busy night and day.*

11.11.87: *The laundry machinery arrived yesterday.*

11.26.87: *The furniture for the new hotel was seen on every boat yesterday bound for the beach.*

11.30.87: *All the Eastern help that has been engaged has been telegraphed for and will arrive here about December 6. They number about 250 persons, 100 of whom will come from Chicago, and the remainder from New York and Philadelphia.*

12.9.87: *The kitchen is nearly completed, and the ranges are already used by the hotel employees.*

12.11.87: *A visitor yesterday remarked on the absence of police protection on the beach. "We don't need them, sir," said an old resident. "We have no saloons or gambling houses, and we have yet to hear of an unlawful act."*

12.12.87: *The hotel is to have a resident physician.*

12.15.87: *The completion of the buildings now under way is being seriously affected by the lime famine; there is none of this building requisite on the market.*

12.21.87: *The theater [Ballroom] is rapidly approaching completion. It will be opened by [a performance from] an Eastern dramatic company.*

12.22.87: *The new ferryboat will have no under cabins. The entire lower deck is to be given over to vehicles.*

12.29.87: *The furniture is now being distributed ... every one of the 250 people, lately arrived from the East as hotel help, are pressed into service.*

12.31.87: *Telegraphic communication from Coronado Beach to all parts of the world will be established.*

1.6.88: *The monthly payroll of the Coronado Beach Company amounted to $32,000. It was divided yesterday among 600 employees.*

1.7.88: *The large hotel annunciator [call bell] system arrived yesterday. It communicates with 630 separate wires.*

1.8.88: *The carpet layers commenced work.*

1.11.88: *The most noticeable event is ... the arrival of Mrs. E.J. Owens of Chicago. This lady is a famous hairdresser from the East, well known to female vanity, and will follow her profession at the hotel in the days to come.*

1.14.88: *The 2,000 barrels of cement recently unloaded ... will be used in the laying of the cement walks on the hotel grounds.*

1.17.88: *Four hundred chandeliers have already been put up in the hotel, and 800 more have yet to be placed.*

1.20.88: *All the windows in the hotel will be shaded with Venetian blinds and draped with coin Swiss curtains.*

1.22.88: *The noon hour is an interesting and amusing time to visitors of the Hotel del Coronado. A steam whistle is heard, and at the first sound every one of the large force drops his or her work instantly. The punctuality with which all work ceases is only exceeded by the promptitude with which everybody hastens for the midday meal.*

1.23.88: *Over 900 granite slabs were unpacked yesterday at the hotel. They are for washstands, bureaus, mantel tops, etc.*

1.26.88: *A large number of applications are made daily by men who want to establish stores or offices in the building. They meet with no encouragement whatever from the managers, it not being their intention to turn the hotel into a bazaar.*

Continued on page 12

FACING PAGE TOP LEFT
Elisha Babcock, Jr., and Hampton Story formed the Coronado Beach Company to develop the island and build the Hotel Del; subsidiaries included water, ferry and railroad companies.

FACING PAGE TOP RIGHT
Much of the wood used in the construction of The Del came from the Northwest, floated down the Pacific in gigantic log rafts.

FACING PAGE BOTTOM
Establishing a San Diego Bay transportation system was paramount for delivering materials and workers. Steam ferries later replaced sailing ships.

CORONADO BEACH,

SAN DIEGO COUNTY, CALIFORNIA.

THE CORONADO BEACH COMPANY

HAS BEEN ORGANIZED WITH A CAPITAL OF ONE MILLION DOLLARS, AND WITH THE FOLLOWING
SUBSIDIARY COMPANIES :

Coronado Water Company	$500,000
San Diego & Coronado Ferry Company	$250,000
Coronado Railroad Company	$500,000

DIRECTORS:

E. S. BABCOCK, JR.   -   San Diego.

H. L. STORY, San Diego (of Story & Clark), Chicago.   JACOB GRUENDIKE, Pres. First Nat. Bank, San Diego.

GILES KELLOGG, Coronado.   H. N. COOK, Coronado

OFFICERS:

E. S. BABCOCK, JR., President.   H. L. STORY, Vice-President   THOS. GARDINER, General Agent.

FIRST NATIONAL BANK, San Diego, Treasurer.

POST OFFICE ADDRESS : CORONADO, CALIFORNIA.

1889.
F. M. Dalmazzo, Printer,
San Diego :

Log Rafts of five million feet each, 900 feet long, depth 28 feet below Waterline, in Harbor.

2.4.88: *The uniforms for the employees of the hotel were unpacked yesterday. The bellboys, messengers and elevator men will be dressed in gray corduroy, trimmed with black, and caps to match.*

2.7.88: *Water was turned on yesterday for the first time on the fountain in the court. It threw a stream 25 feet high.*

2.8.88: *The passenger elevator at the Hotel del Coronado made trial trips yesterday. Everything worked smoothly and no hitches occurred.*

2.13.88: *The paintings, steel engravings and etchings, which will decorate the rooms of the hotel, were unpacked yesterday. Their number is legion, and it can easily be seen that they have been selected by a connoisseur.*

2.15.88: *The reading and smoking room ... is provided with leading journals from all parts of the world.*

2.20.88: *The first dinner was served yesterday in the grand dining room of the Hotel del Coronado. This vast and elegant room, with its wealth of appointments, is a rare sight, especially under the brilliant incandescent lights that illuminate it. The polished floors over which an army of trained servants noiselessly glide, the high inlaid ceilings, the snowy linen and the glitter of the silver and glassware combined make a most charming picture. The room may have its equal, but it certainly is not surpassed anywhere.*

For additional construction information, please refer to
Building the Dream: The Design and Construction of the Hotel del Coronado.

RIGHT
A great deal of lumber was used in the construction of the hotel; unfortunately, the amount needed was not as much as estimated, and after The Del was completed, Babcock tried to unload "about three million feet" in Los Angeles and San Diego markets.

RIGHT INSET
Plumber Henry Simpson (center) working on The Del in 1887.

FOLLOWING PAGE
The hotel's construction required the establishment of a number of support services, including an electrical power plant. Electricity was still a novelty in 1888, and the Hotel del Coronado was thought to be one of the largest buildings in the country to have been "electrified." The Del — which also supplied electricity to the city of Coronado — waxed poetic in its 1888 brochure: "Darkness soon bids fair to become unknown in Coronado."

TOP AND BOTTOM LEFT
*A streetcar carried tourists from the Coronado ferry landing
to the construction site, where they enjoyed the beach and
watched the resort's progress.*

BOTTOM RIGHT
*For San Diegans, the construction of the big hotel — a ferry
ride away — offered an ideal Sunday outing.*

The Woman in the Window

The Hotel del Coronado's most prominent stained-glass window — located on the front façade — garners a great deal of attention from visitors, who are curious about the window's lineage and female likeness.

Original to the hotel, the window was first mounted in the massive lobby chimney, visible from the front exterior as well as from the lobby interior. After the fireplace was removed in the 1920s, the stained glass was displayed at The Del in a variety of interior locations. In 1995, it was moved to its present exterior fourth-floor site, above the porte cochere.

The figure is frequently believed to be a depiction of the mythical goddess Queen Calafia (the accent is on the third syllable), from whom the name California is thought to derive, and the crown and sunburst are believed to symbolize California's 19th-century emergence as a state blessed with golden riches. The artwork also features the great seal of California.

But a November 2, 1887, *San Diego Union* article, which referenced the hotel's contract for stained glass (reportedly designed by architect James Reid), may be more accurate:

> The largest piece will be an allegorical representation of Coronado. In the foreground is the figure of a young girl, crowning herself with flowers and scattering them about. In the distant background there is a landscape, representing mountains, valleys and a bay. The sun is just rising above a high elevation. Around the figure in panels there are representations of the various resources of California. This piece of stained glass will alone cost $600. It will be placed over the large mantel in the office.

That this is not an accurate description of the completed stained-glass may be the reason a later issue of the *Union*, on February 17, 1888, contained a less detailed reference: "One of the principal features of the gallery is the large stained-glass window, which represents 'Coronation' in rich colors."

ABOVE
According to architect James Reid, construction on The Del began on the least complicated front and proceeded to the more complex side (shown above); this schedule allowed the mostly unskilled workforce to gain competence as they progressed.

RIGHT
A c. 1888 promotional piece boasted that the hotel "enjoys the distinction of covering more ground than any other hotel in the world." Despite the Del's sprawling footprint, this claim may have been unfounded.

CORONADO BEACH

CALIFORNIA.

Open for Business

Notably absent from the Hotel del Coronado's early history is an "official" opening day, although February 19 — the day the hotel served its first meal in the main dining room — is often credited as The Del's birthday. In reality, guests began checking into the hotel on January 26, according to a *San Diego Union* article the next day:

> The following persons registered at the Hotel del Coronado yesterday: Miss L. White, Seymour, Ind.; Samuel E. Berry, Del Mar; Joseph Davis and family, Helena, Montana; Mrs. Van Immagen, Beloit, Wis.; C.J. Sterling, Los Angeles; James L. Mason, Greenfield, Ind.; Miss Mollie St. Julian, Indianapolis, Ind.; Chester Snider, Kansas City.

Perhaps because none of these guests had name recognition, the first "official" guests — as reported in the *San Diego Union* on January 29 — checked in on January 28:

> A suite of nine rooms was prepared at the Hotel del Coronado yesterday for occupation by Nelson Morris, the great cattle king, and Don A. Sweet, assistant to the Vice-President of the Atchison, Topeka and Santa Fe railroad. They will be the first guests to place their names on the register of this hotel.

In the fashion of the times, the Nelson Morris party enjoyed a lengthy stay, departing on March 13 for Pasadena, probably en route to another resort retreat.

Meanwhile, hotel advertisements in the *Los Angeles Times* specified: "Opened to Receive Guests February 15, 1888" (these were published between March 9 and April 9). In reality, according to a *San Diego Union* article on January 25, "The first guest to be accommodated at the hotel is James W. Reid, architect of the mammoth [hotel], who moved into the building last week."

Babcock himself seemed uncertain *when* the Hotel del Coronado should publicly commemorate its opening. In a letter dated February 21, 1888, he wrote, "As soon as the date is decided upon for the opening of the hotel ... you will see [it] in the papers." As late as April, a date still hadn't been determined.

Although the official opening of the hotel seemed permanently delayed, The Del's opening season was successful enough, according to a letter Babcock wrote on February 27, 1888: "...it might be of interest for you to know that though the hotel is not finished, and we only opened the doors to those who insisted on coming, we had, last evening, at dinner over 500 guests and the arrivals on Saturday last were over 100. We have now about 400, and the guests are coming faster than they go."

HOTEL DEL CORONADO.

J. B. SEGHERS, JR., MANAGER.

CORONADO, - - - - CALIFORNIA.

Setting the Scene: San Diego Circa 1888

When the Hotel del Coronado opened in 1888, the city of San Diego was one of its biggest promoters. In fact, a San Diego brochure (15-page, hardcover booklet) devoted more than five pages to describing the city's newest and most noteworthy asset.

But before focusing on the Hotel del Coronado, this sales piece extolled the virtues of San Diego, calling out "its matchless climate ... surpassing that of the most famous health resorts of Europe ... a perpetual source of wonder to visitors." San Diego was praised for being neither too hot ("entirely free from what is known in the Eastern cities as 'the heated term'"), nor too cold ("a 'cold spell' is equally unknown").

San Diego's "remarkable fertility of the land" was also lauded, with the "wonderful capacity of the soil for fruit growing," boasting, "Tomatoes bear for three years on the same vines. Strawberries and other small fruits will pay better than a gold mine."

Hailed as California's first European settlement, San Diego was described as a "beautiful little city, which may properly be called the Gem of the Coast," and likened to Naples, "gradually sloping down to the bay." There was also a "magnificent harbor ... sufficient upon which to build a great city ... there is no safer harbor on the Pacific coast."

Although the brochure called out three "large" hotels in downtown San Diego — Horton House, Florence and The St. James — these well-appointed hostelries (100–150 rooms each) were dwarfed by the Hotel del Coronado's size and expansive setting.

The Hotel del Coronado

With the formation of the Coronado Beach Company "organized for the purpose of erecting and conducting the Hotel del Coronado, which it was determined should be constructed, furnished and conducted regardless of expense," the famed hotel was characterized as a "mammoth structure" with "a picturesque diversity of architectural display."

Continued on page 22

RIGHT

Clara Wood Bunker, who was born in 1846, completed this pencil sketch of The Del during a c. 1890 visit. The Bunker family lived and ran a business in Oceanside, California, and traveled to Coronado for summer outings.

According to a hotel brochure:

> The site of the Hotel del Coronado occupies twenty acres upon a peninsula, which is almost surrounded [by water] ... connected to the city of San Diego by ferry. The waves of the Pacific wash the foot of the terraced bluff in front of the hotel, and the scene presented is one of picturesque and grand beauty.

Public Rooms

The brochure also described additional lobby-level public spaces, including a ladies' billiard room ("handsomely carpeted with Wilton"), writing and reading room, smoking and chess room, ladies' reception room and music room with a "grand upright piano" ("a beautiful mantel in the room is symbolical of music, being carved in musical designs, while the walls are decorated with pictures and etchings of famous musicians and composers").

In the lower lobby area, there were three card rooms "neatly fitted up," as well as ladies' and gentlemen's bathing rooms ("both salt and freshwater and Turkish baths") and ladies' and gentlemen's "hair dressing" rooms. There was also a "gents' furnishing store," drugstore and four "85-feet bowling alleys, two of which are reserved especially for ladies."

Grounds and Gardens

At the center of the Hotel del Coronado was a "grand court, 150 by 250 feet, with a fountain in the center, illuminated with incandescent lights," and planted with almond, fig, loquat, lime, olive, banana, guava, lemon, orange and pomegranate trees, along with "tropical plants and flowers ... affording a scene found in no other hotel in the world."

Electric Lights

Although this early San Diego brochure generously praised The Del, it did not mention its impressive electrical system; however, a hotel brochure from that time referenced its "Mather incandescent electric lamps, of which there are 2,500." In addition, annunciators provided an internal communication system between guestrooms and hotel offices.

"No Small Undertaking"

San Diego's promotional brochure concluded its tribute to the Hotel del Coronado with an enthusiastic endorsement of the structure itself, as well as the vision of its founders, Elisha Babcock, Jr., and Hampton Story.

> Even from the foregoing description and figures, only an imperfect comprehension of the magnitude and beauty of such a structure as the Hotel del Coronado can be obtained. Neither is the vast amount of the capital invested nor the nerve it takes to invest the same comprehended by people who have never left the populous centers of the East and traveled thousands of miles to the Pacific Coast, and there found on our distant western shores a hotel that not only rivals but far surpasses any hotel on the Atlantic Coast.

> When the thousands of tourists flock to the Golden State this coming winter and reach Coronado Beach, they will no doubt be greatly astonished to find not simply a hotel of unprecedented magnitude, elegance, beauty and convenience, but one managed on a scale of liberality and style never before attempted in an American tourists' hotel.

A Healthy Holiday

Aside from The Del's aesthetic attributes and technological advances, Victorian travelers were drawn to the hotel's Southern California location, known for its health-inducing sunshine and restorative ocean air and water. An 1888 Hotel Del brochure detailed the advantages of Coronado in a section titled "Comparison of the Mean Temperature at Mediterranean Resorts with Coronado," in which The Del was shown to have a superior climate to "five of the world-renowned sanitariums and most popular European resorts [Naples, Mentone, Rome, Nice and Florence]."

The brochure continued: "Coronado has the most equable temperature known among the dwelling places of civilized men on the face of the globe. Here we breathe the true elixir of life and fear none of those insidious maladies so prevalent and fatal in most localities." A doctor quoted in the brochure testified that cholera, scarlet fever, diphtheria, measles, whooping cough and tuberculosis were practically unknown.

The Hotel del Coronado also promoted its drinking water — which was piped in from San Diego — as a "mineral water" health amenity (and many doctors offered testimonials on its behalf). An 1888 advertisement in the *Los Angeles Times* boasted of The Del's "abundance of pure and palatable water, which has superior qualities ... excellent in kidney troubles."

PAGES 24–25
The hotel, which cost an estimated $600,000 to build and $400,000 to furnish, was a technological marvel in its day: It was lighted by electricity, heated by a combination of steam and fireplaces, and featured elevators and telephones.

Pacific Perfection

An early brochure listed "What There Is and What There Is Not at Coronado":

There is:

The most equable climate in the world.
Perfect sanitation.
Perfectly pure water.
Perfectly pure ice.
Plenty of sunlight.
Cool nights.
The most picturesque environment on the Pacific Coast.

There is not:

Any hay fever.
Any malaria.
Any sleeplessness.
Any loss of appetite.
Any languor in the air.
A "heated term" or a "cold snap."

For "What One Can Do at Coronado," the brochure suggested a number of hunting, fishing and sightseeing excursions, along with more close-by enjoyments:

Take a "constitutional" along the beach before breakfast.
A sunning on the south veranda afterwards.
A spin on the bay before dinner and afterwards.
A *siesta* in one of the easy-chairs in the glass-enclosed gallery.
Dance in the evening.
Enjoy a *dolce far niente* in the sand in the afternoon.
Promenade the iron pier.
Dip into the surf.
Gather some of the beautiful shells found along the beach.
Lose one's self in the Labyrinth.
Attend the concerts.
Spend an hour a day in the Museum.
Hire a donkey for a jog along the shore.
Go to the theater.
Taste the luxury of a hot seawater plunge bath.
Enjoy about the best things of life generally.

ABOVE
The brochure included this picture of an oceanfront veranda with a superimposed couple — in all their finery — gazing out to sea.

Original Employee Hugh Francis Griffin

Handsome Hugh F. Griffin was one of The Del's first employees, an accomplished hotel man from back East, who was hired as a front-office clerk for $60 a month (an impressive salary in its day). His first letter on Del stationery is dated 1887, before the hotel opened, when the 22-year-old surmised, "I think this will be the most beautiful spot in the world, and the hotel the finest." On January 19, 1888, Griffin offered a two-week status report: "I can only say that I am more than satisfied, I am contented. The change [giving up his job at the Bartholdi Hotel in New York] was a risk, the long journey a severe undertaking, yet ... all our pain and trouble is not without some reward."

On February 8, Griffin provided an update to his family back East: "We are opened for business here now, and have quite a number of guests; still the house and grounds will not be in proper shape for another month. There are a number of novel things to be seen at this place, in and about the hotel, all the rooms are lighted up with electric light ... it seems rather odd to go to your room and turn on the light, just as you would gas, and besides it saves all the trouble and annoyance of matches, and can be turned on or off at leisure. I have one of the prettiest little rooms you ever saw, with a fine sycamore bed, dresser, washstand, rocker, two chairs, and one of the nicest carpets imaginable. The taste displayed in furnishing the whole house is of the very best, and in fact, all the appointments are carried out in a first-class style. From all accounts, you people back East are having a very cold winter; we here have the same warm weather, day in and day out."

Other letters and observations followed:

February 24: "I am writing this under difficulties. The band is playing in the rotunda of the office, and with all the noise and confusion I can scarcely form my thoughts to know what I am saying."

March 19: "Everything is in running order here now. I work from ten o'clock in the morning till twelve o'clock at night, except two hours in the afternoon when I go fishing (and that sport is simply great here)." In fact, a February 28 article in the *San Diego Union* reported, "H.F. Griffin of the Hotel del Coronado is an enthusiast in all matters concerning boating and is endeavoring to organize a boat club here." Griffin's letter continued, "I am writing this as the infernal band is playing, and it's no easy job. The weather here is one day after another, all warmth and sunshine ... I never enjoyed better health in my life than I do now and am very glad I came here if for nothing but to build myself into a man."

Birds eye View

THIS PAGE TOP
The hotel's Queen Anne architecture was once characterized as a cross between an ornate wedding cake and a well-trimmed ship, a description that captured both the whimsy and commanding presence of The Del.

THIS PAGE BOTTOM
At the time the hotel was built, it was entirely encircled by verandas, estimated to be more than 7,000 feet combined.

FACING PAGE TOP
The Garden Patio was at the heart of the hotel's design, and early brochures made much of its generous proportions (150 by 250 feet) and exotic plants.

FACING PAGE BOTTOM LEFT
A c. 1888 picture included a photographer at work.

FACING PAGE BOTTOM RIGHT
In the early days, visitors were brought to San Diego by a new transcontinental railroad connection. The hotel's ferry system ("the trip across the bay occupies only four minutes") transported guests from San Diego to its wharves in Coronado, where visitors were conveyed to The Del in private horse-drawn carriages or by streetcar.

FOLLOWING PAGE
An early promotional rendering of The Del included a flock of seagulls. A lengthy text on the reverse side highlighted the hotel's "refreshing restfulness."

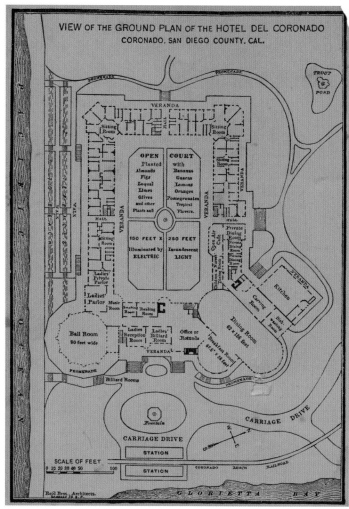

Court, Hotel Del Coronado.

207.

Hotel del Coronado, San Diego County, California.

TURNER'S ELITE STUDIO, COR. FIFTH AND F STS., SAN DIEGO, CAL.

LARGEST COLLECTION OF VIEWS IN THE CITY

Hotel Del Coronado From

Through the Years

A Historic Perspective

The years between 1888 and 1919 took the Hotel del Coronado from the Victorian period into the modern age. When the hotel opened, the Victorian period was nearing its official end (England's Queen Victoria, who began her reign in 1837, would die in 1901); yet much of the world remained the same, including everyday life for well-to-do Americans.

It wasn't until Europe entered World War I in 1914 that the days of Victoriana began to wane, and many historians consider the first decade of the 20th century so representative of the Victorian era that they sometimes refer to those years as "the last decade of the 19th century." But by the time World War I ended in 1918, everything had shifted: America had come of age as a world power and emerged a world leader, eclipsing even England (most tellingly, America no longer identified its own historic time periods with the names of British monarchs).

Tough Times for The Del

The Del in 1888 was a decidedly Victorian-era seaside resort, designed to attract elite travelers from around the world. In typical Victorian fashion, the hotel offered a healthy destination (sunny climate, near the sea), which appealed to upper-class Victorians, and it offered every state-of-the-art amenity, which a wealthy clientele demanded.

Unfortunately, while The Del was poised for success, San Diego was not: The real estate boom of 1885 had burst in 1887, and San Diego was no longer an up-and-coming city; it was a city in decline. Those who had invested in San Diego real estate were left without an economy with which to support themselves, and the city's population quickly plummeted from 35,000 to 16,000 people.

In Coronado, land purchasers defaulted on loans held by founders Elisha Babcock, Jr., and Hampton Story, who in turn were unable to pay *their* creditors, and Babcock's early correspondence is filled with letters asking for money owed, while imploring his lenders to be lenient. This financial shortfall, coupled with added construction costs — notably, the expense of building a rail line around the bay, connecting the hotel directly to San Diego's depot — left Babcock and Story strapped.

John D. Spreckels to the Rescue

Fortunately, John D. Spreckels, a wealthy San Francisco businessman, was smitten with San Diego and had begun investing in the city as early as 1887. He was known to Babcock and Story (who may have used his ships to transport building materials from Northern California), and they turned to him for financial assistance, which he provided, most likely before the hotel even opened. This arrangement continued for a number of years, after which Spreckels assumed ownership of the Hotel del Coronado, retaining Babcock as manager.

With Spreckels' financial backing, The Del was able to survive San Diego's shrinking economy, as well as an 1893 nationwide depression, after which the economic tide began to turn as Spreckels' investment continued. In 1900, Spreckels created Tent City, modest camping accommodations south of the hotel, as a way to appeal to America's emerging middle-class clientele (see pages 134–147). In addition, he instituted polo in 1906, attracting scores of wealthy guests, and added a private hotel school in 1913 to serve the children of long-term visitors.

Under Spreckels' ownership, the hotel promoted the development of a military base (in part to expand Coronado's economy), and in 1911 Glenn Hammond Curtiss made the first successful amphibian flight. Spreckels also saw the arrival of President Theodore Roosevelt's "Great White Fleet," 16 battleships that anchored off The Del in 1908:

> *What excitement! The hotel was bursting with old braid and high silk hats. All day and night it was busy with high officers or civilian dignitaries going to and from the ships. Everything was done in high protocol.*

In a never-ceasing effort to expand Coronado's cultural and economic base, Spreckels leased land to Lubin Movie Studios in 1915

Continued on page 34

for only $1 a year, with the stipulation that all studio employees reside in Coronado. Although the studio's tenure was short-lived, Siegmund Lubin made as many as 20 movies in Coronado before his film production business folded.

After the 1906 San Francisco earthquake, Spreckels moved his family to Coronado, becoming a major player in the San Diego business community, where he founded and oversaw everything from newspapers to streetcar lines.

A Banner Season

During the Spreckels' years, the Hotel del Coronado became a secure fixture in San Diego society and a major destination in its own right. And with the 1915 Panama-California Exposition — celebrating the 1914 completion of the Panama Canal — The Del's guest register read like a society who's who, with former President Taft, Thomas Edison and Henry Ford stopping by.

Other hotel guests that year included the Frederick K. Vanderbilts, who traveled to San Diego aboard their yacht via the Panama Canal. Relatives from another millionaire family, the Edwin Goulds, arrived in more historic fashion: on their own private railcar.

World War I

The war in Europe (declared in 1914) drew more visitors to The Del, as the nearby aviation field stepped up training for possible American involvement. Since many officers came from prominent American families, a 1915 edition of *The California* went to great lengths to list the hotel's resident admirals and their relations, including young Tommy Morton, namesake grandson of Admiral Thomas Benton Howard, who "corrected an ignorant grownup" by asking to be called by his Navy family's pet name, "Commodore."

Even before America entered the war in 1917, the Navy's Pacific Fleet was ever-present, and as the war in Europe raged on, The Del extended the hand of friendship to nearby North Island. This resulted in a kind of wartime social whirl, with The Del at the center of a privileged society scene (which the *San Diego Union* described as "gay with military uniforms"). Among other things, the hotel hosted a tea for all Coronado officers and their ladies; sent 1,000 Tent City entertainment tickets to 600 Marines aboard the *USS South Dakota*; offered its guests the privilege of viewing regimental parades twice weekly at North Island ("nowhere in America can aviation be seen to such advantage"); and hosted six admirals, including the commander-in-chief of the Pacific Fleet, at its 1916 Leap Year Ball.

After America joined the fight, life at The Del took a more serious turn: "Meatless" and "wheatless" meals were instituted (to conserve for the troops), and an ad in the daily program at Tent City proclaimed, "You Can Help Win the War — Eat Less Food." Thrift

stamps (which raised funds for the war) were sold in hotel offices, and guests were encouraged to donate wool, money, books — and anything else — to Coronado's Red Cross.

According to one account, knitting bags were brought to all 1918 Del social events so guests could continue their efforts making sweaters and socks for the troops. Hotel concerts and balls were held to benefit units overseas or for the relief of French and Belgian widows and orphans; and Tent City guests contributed more than $2,400 in 1918, when evening concerts were filled with patriotic songs and military marches.

FACING PAGE
Mrs. Henry Stephens II of Grosse Pointe, Michigan, visited The Del c. 1890 with her sister, Marion, and her son, Henry Stephen III, who was born in 1883.

THIS PAGE ABOVE
A turn-of-the-century fire drill.

THIS PAGE ABOVE
A group of guests, c. 1900.

FACING PAGE TOP
This photo of an ocean-side veranda was included in an 1888 Hotel Del brochure. Verandas — today considered an architectural amenity — were a Victorian necessity, providing fresh air without direct exposure to the sun.

FACING PAGE MIDDLE
Some stylish Del guests pose in the Garden Patio, c. 1900.

FACING PAGE BOTTOM
This photo was probably taken in front of the Garden Patio fountain, which was said to be surrounded by calla lilies.

135. Hotel Del Coronado Varanda - faceing Ocean.

Noel at The Del in 1892

In 1892, a young girl named Noel arrived at the hotel with her parents and young brother for the winter season, from January to April — a typical time period for well-to-do Eastern guests. During their visit, Noel wrote letters to her "little cousins in the East," which were accompanied by beautiful pencil and water-color artwork that may have been drawn by Noel's "nurse" (at that time, nannies were schooled in the arts so they could educate their young charges).

This collection of letters and drawings was in the hands of a private collector before it was purchased by the Hotel del Coronado, after which it was published in the book *"The Loveliest Hotel You Can Imagine": A Child's View of the Hotel del Coronado According to Letters and Drawings from Her 1892 Visit.*

Noel was enthusiastic in her description of The Del:

> This is the loveliest, biggest hotel you can imagine. It has ever and ever so many funny little windows and balconies like the big dovecote at Grandma's. The hotel is white and has red roofs everywhere. The red and the white between the bluest sky and the bluest water is like a beautiful dream in a fairy story. The hotel is built around a lovely garden, which is called a court. In the middle of it is a fountain, around which grows a wreath of calla lilies. I never saw so many calla lilies together at once, not even in church on Easter Day.

Noel was especially intrigued by Coronado's ostrich farm (but not in a good way!):

> I do not like ostriches; they are so homely. They have no feathers on their long legs or on their long necks. When they are angry their eyes turn red, and they hiss and put out their tongues like a snake. P.S. I forgot to tell you, sometimes ostriches roar like lions.

Vincent Surr, Bootblack to a Vice President, 1893

Edward Vincent Surr, who was born in London in 1870, moved to San Diego with his family in 1884, arriving in New York and traveling by train to California. Ultimately, his parents became prominent in San Diego society — Joseph was the British vice consul; Elizabeth lectured at the National History Society — but in the interim, Vincent had to earn a living ("there are vicissitudes in life").

In 1893, Surr (who went by his middle name, Vincent) was newly hired as a bootblack at the Hotel del Coronado, where he recorded his observations of visiting Vice President Adlai Stevenson (to Grover Cleveland) in an essay titled *Against the Grain: An Anglo-California's Experience*:

> My bootblack stand is in the barbershop, and it is here that I meet Vice President Stevenson the morning after his arrival. And while the barber is occupied with that worthy [personage], my attention is fairly well occupied by the lower extremities of a senator or two. Consequently, my recollections of the great man are rather mixed and consist principally of a figure swathed in a barber's sheet, from which some kind of head emerged.

Surr also functioned as a porter, a job that began at 6 a.m. and required much sweeping, cleaning ("an acre or two of basement") and wheeling of trunks. With breakfast and "a hasty lunch" provided, Surr was free from 3 to 5:30 p.m. After supper, he was back on duty until 8 p.m., when "a further respite is granted until 10 p.m.," after which he was "once more expected to appear upon the scene and hold himself in readiness."

In a memoir written in 1924, Surr recorded his ever-increasing responsibilities as a Hotel Del employee:

> "Surr," he [Babcock] said, "I have been watching you. You've got brains, and I am going to make a place for you in the general office." In all my subsequent life, no compliment has meant as much to me as that from this man. And so I found myself in "the Beach office," and in the intervals between reading meters and collecting water bills, I was engaged in reading "postings" which were copied from journals and cashbooks into mysterious ledgers.

> He saw my sincerity and commented that I was the sort of material the company needed, and I remained to serve the company for, in all, nearly seven years. As my knowledge increased, so my duties varied and expanded.

> Suffice it to say that E.S. Babcock, the then manager of the Spreckels' interests, was a great man, equal to five ordinary men ... [and] for nearly seven years I poured out faithful energy in his employ. It may be that he inspired us. I think there was something in the heights to which he should have attained that led me to get the best out of myself.

> I [was appointed] to the Board of Directors of two or three companies, was secretary of several of them, was buyer for them, and was acting superintendent of the ferry and of the Coronado Railroad. I was also private secretary to the President [Elisha Babcock].

> All of these honors meant very little in dollars and cents. I never got beyond one hundred dollars monthly to support my family, which had increased to include four children ... working through Saturday afternoon and all day Sunday, frequently leaning back from my Remington typewriter ... [with] absolute fatigue that I might be abreast of the hundred letters or so that he had saddled me with. The mail was always very heavy.

Surr was employed by the Hotel del Coronado from 1893 to 1900. After his first wife died, he married again and moved to Australia, before settling in San Francisco, where he studied and practiced law. Vincent Surr died in 1951.

ABOVE
The Surr residence — where Vincent, his parents and other family members lived during their years in Coronado — is still standing, looking much as it did in this turn-of-the-century painting, rendered by Vincent's sister, Jane Morin Surr Krause, whose work was later exhibited at the Louvre Museum in Paris.

TOP
A c. 1901 hotel brochure highlighted The Del's wonderful weather and outdoor activities, but it also spoke to a resort's inherent sociability: "You will find all kinds of flowers at Coronado but not wallflowers — unsociable people."

BOTTOM LEFT
By 1904 or so, the hotel's trees had grown tall in California's warm Mediterranean-type climate.

BOTTOM RIGHT
In 1904, the Hotel del Coronado unveiled the first electrically lit, outdoor living Christmas tree.

ABOVE
Guests in the Garden Patio, c. 1905. In the top photo, note the woman to the far right facing the figure in the fountain to the far left.

RIGHT
A drawing of The Del's Garden Patio from a turn-of-the-century brochure.

SAN DIEGO HARBOR IMPROVEMENTS

Bird's Eye View of San Diego, the Harbor and Coronado Beach.

THIS PAGE
Pictures from c. 1910 include a drawing of Coronado and the San Diego Harbor (top), a fire drill in progress (middle) and a group gathering (bottom).

FACING PAGE TOP
An unidentified woman poses in front of the hotel.

FACING PAGE BOTTOM LEFT
The family in front of The Del are the Olneys, with sons Bud (blond) and Jack. The boys' father owned the first hardware store in Coronado, and the youngsters spent a lot of time at Tent City. Bud later reported, "The hotel was a place that I admired and was envious of because I never got to go inside until I was an adult."

FACING PAGE MIDDLE RIGHT
The woman in the fashionable black hat, with the hotel in the distant background, is Mrs. Joseph Charles (Frances Heading Lindley) Muehe, who honeymooned at The Del in 1909. Frances' family were pioneer citrus ranchers; her husband, Joseph, hailed from a prominent Portland, Oregon, family, eventually becoming president of the First National Bank of Azusa, California.

FACING PAGE BOTTOM RIGHT
An early photo of the hotel's front landscaping.

G. Aubrey Davidson: Hotel Resident and San Diegan Extraordinaire

Prominent San Diego businessman G. Aubrey Davidson, who conceived the city's Panama-California Exposition — to coincide with the completion of the Panama Canal in 1914 — was a longtime resident of the hotel, where he entertained a glittering social circle, including Franklin and Eleanor Roosevelt. After founding San Diego's Southern Trust & Savings Bank (a forerunner of Bank of America), Davidson became active in the Chamber of Commerce, where he proposed:

> For twenty years, this organization, and the entire Pacific Coast, has waited for the building of the Panama Canal. It occurs to me that the opening should be the signal for San Diego to put on a great celebration, not just a county or state fair, but an international exposition.

A lifelong supporter of all things San Diego, Davidson had arrived in the city in 1886, when he was just 18 (he was reportedly on hand for the Hotel Del's groundbreaking). Davidson fell in love with the locale but bemoaned the fact that "there's no city to go with it." He started his career at the Santa Fe Railway, with a short stint in Los Angeles, after which he returned to San Diego, established his banking business and became one of the city's leading lenders, helping to jump-start San Diego's fledgling economy.

Davidson's proposal for a 1915 world's fair was designed to attract visitors to San Diego, while providing the city with a cultivated and culturally rich center-city park. As California's first port en route from the Panama Canal, the exposition slogan became "The Land Divided — the World United; San Diego the First Port of Call."

By the time the exposition opened, Davidson was president of the organization and living at the Hotel del Coronado with his wife and son, where he entertained an impressive list of visitors, including President Howard Taft, Thomas Edison, Franklin Roosevelt (then Assistant Secretary of the Navy) and England's Prince of Wales. A 1916 *San Diego Union* article described Davidson as "imperturbable in temperament, polished in manner, quietly, if not slowly, spoken." Davidson's long association with Franklin Roosevelt — along with his own desire to establish San Diego as a Navy port — was instrumental in the development of Naval Air Station North Island.

After the 1915 exposition, Davidson became an advocate for the preservation of the Balboa Park buildings (which were intended to be temporary). So successful was his campaign that restoration work begun in 1933 prompted another San Diego exposition in 1935, the California-Pacific International Exposition, for which Davidson served as chairman of the board, giving him the opportunity to entertain President and Mrs. Roosevelt at his Hotel del Coronado home.

Davidson, a visionary San Diego businessman, was also committed to the city's past, and when Balboa Park exposition buildings were once again threatened in 1947, he became the first chairman of the Balboa Park Restoration Committee.

He was also an active supporter of the Army and Navy YMCA, securing funds for its building in 1923, which served thousands of men during World War II.

In 1948, Davidson was on hand to celebrate the 60th birthday of the Hotel del Coronado, where he had lived with his family for a couple of decades. Davidson's son, Gilbert, followed his parents' example, residing at the hotel with his family during the 1940s and 1950s.

Soon after the hotel's 60th birthday celebration, Davidson's residential reign at the hotel ended, by which time he had also retired from his professional life. In his later years, Davidson received accolades for his business, civic and military contributions and was named the "First Citizen of San Diego." Another fitting tribute came from a San Diego Convention Bureau manager who said, "While others were building local institutions, Davidson was making a national institution out of San Diego." Davidson was also honored as "the man who brought the Navy to San Diego," receiving the Navy's highest civilian award, the Distinguished Service Medal, in 1956.

When G. Aubrey Davidson died in 1957 at age 89, his death was front-page news for the *San Diego Evening Tribune*, which proclaimed, "His Work Helped Build Community into Metropolis."

ABOVE LEFT
G. Aubrey Davidson (center) entertaining Henry Ford (right) and brother Edsel during the 1915 Panama-California Exposition.

13574 RESIDENCE OF MR. JOHN D. SPRECKELS, CORONADO BEACH CALIF

TOP LEFT
This c. 1915 photo shows an era in transition, when traditional horse-drawn carriages shared the driveway with automobiles.

TOP RIGHT
A Panama-California Exposition decal featured the Hotel del Coronado.

MIDDLE
By 1915, John D. Spreckels (left), the hotel's second owner, was a preeminent San Diego businessman and in residence in Coronado (right).

BOTTOM
This c. 1915 photo of a hotel painter posing on the roof was actually a postcard, perhaps to appeal to the exposition tourists who frequented The Del.

FOR THE BENEFIT OF HOMELESS LADIES IN FRANCE
WHO HAVE FLED FROM THE WAR ZONE

THE MANAGEMENT OF

HOTEL DEL CORONADO

REQUESTS THE PLEASURE OF YOUR PRESENCE

ON TUESDAY, JANUARY 30, 1917, AT 8:30 P. M. *Tonight*

In the ball room

DRAMATIC STUDIES OF ROMAN CHARACTERS, BY

MR. S. RICHARD FULLER

"CLEOPATRA AND HER CHILDREN"

AFTER THE LECTURE ANY SUMS FOR THIS CAUSE MAY BE
PLACED IN THE BASKET AT THE DOOR

ABOVE
*This may have been a military exercise for the benefit
of hotel guests, c. 1917.*

LEFT
*In 1917, the Hotel Del was actively involved in raising
money for European war relief.*

TODAY

At
Hotel del Coronado
Wednesday, August Sixth
Nineteen Nineteen

TOP

In 1919, the cover of the hotel's daily program featured thumbnail sketches of Navy ships. Inside were these lines from Lord Byron:

> She bears her down majestically near
> Speed on her prow, and terror in her tier.
> She walks the waters like a thing of life
> And seems to dare the elements to strife.

The program also included an announcement that "thrift stamps are on sale all the time at the office" (these raised funds for the war effort). Two upcoming social events were mentioned: a dance "in honor of the Pacific Fleet" and a banquet, ball and reception honoring Secretary of the Navy Josephus Daniels, along with other Navy officers and western state governors. With the hotel as busy as it was during World War I, the management suggested "to the ladies in particular that they exercise more care in looking after their furs and wraps. A number of sightseers visit the hotel daily, and it is impossible for us to be responsible for the acts of everyone."

BOTTOM

During World War I, nearby North Island provided a skyward spectacle for hotel guests, who enjoyed watching some of the nation's first pilots take off and land. In this c. 1918 photo, hotel guest Lillian Noble Keene (1880–1953) is shown with Walter Lees (1887–1957), head instructor at the Curtiss Flying School; the plane is a Curtiss Flying Boat Model F. Lees, who had learned to fly at North Island, was a civilian instructor during World War I and later set the world's flying endurance record of 84.5 hours (unrefueled) in 1931. Keene, who came from a well-to-do Chicago family before settling into a 7,600-square-foot mansion in Libertyville, Illinois (complete with a gardener's cottage, barn, clubhouse and two swimming pools), was the chief executive officer for her family's trophy and jewelry manufacturing business. The Curtiss Flying Boat had two seats, which allowed a student — or other favored folk — to fly with an instructor.

1920s

After World War I — and still under the direction of John D. Spreckels — the Hotel del Coronado entered the glittering decade of the 1920s, with a sparkling social life that reflected the celebratory spirit of postwar Americans.

Parties prevailed, resulting in some of the most stylish invitations and menus the hotel ever produced. Prohibition, which had been instituted in 1919, might have put a crimp in the hotel's 1920s social life ... but it didn't seem to: Some speculated that liquor was brought in from nearby Mexico, if not by the hotel, then by its guests.

The 1920s also produced two legendary San Diego banquets, both held in the hotel's Crown Room: one in 1920 for Edward, England's Prince of Wales, who arrived aboard the warship *HMS Renown* (see pages 192; 198–199), and the other in 1927 to honor Charles Lindbergh after the completion of his successful transatlantic flight (see pages 192; 200–201). After Edward's banquet — at which he reportedly questioned his American dinner companion, Mrs. Claus Spreckels, Jr., about the latest Hollywood gossip — the prince was entertained at a grand dance in the Ballroom. For Charles Lindbergh's lavish dinner, a small replica of his plane, *The Spirit of St. Louis*, circled the Crown Room, suspended from the massive ceiling.

A testament to the prosperity and popularity of The Del in the 1920s can also be found in a hotel brochure from that time, which was 32 pages long and featured dozens of finely reproduced photographs. The text highlighted various hotel activities, along with a range of local "amusements and attractions [accessible] over paved roads for motor enthusiasts" (an ever-increasing population). A "first-class garage ... under thoroughly experienced management" assured guests that their vehicles would be well cared for.

The Great Depression and World War II

The stock market crash in 1929 devastated American pocketbooks, after which World War II continued to take its toll on the country's economy and morale. Times were tough at The Del during the Depression, probably made worse by the fact that John D. Spreckels had died in 1926 and was no longer able to invest capital into the project he had so long favored. Fortunately, the Hotel Del — along with Spreckels' other vast holdings — went into trust for his children, where it stayed until 1948. With this extended Spreckels' family tenure — spanning 60 years — the hotel was stable enough to survive the Depression and World War II, events that were the undoing of many other American resorts.

Although it's uncertain how involved Spreckels' descendants were in daily operations or even in year-in, year-out oversight, by 1934, The Del — which had been reportedly losing $100,000 a year (and

on one day in 1933 had only nine occupied guestrooms) — was entrusted to manager Stephen Royce. An acclaimed hotelier from Pasadena, where he owned, managed and lived in the Huntington Hotel, Royce also owned the Fairmont in San Francisco. When he was hired, Royce was contracted for a salary and a percentage of any loss less than $100,000 a year, and according to his son Danny, when the Hotel Del began to see a profit after three years, Royce's contract with the Spreckels Company was rewritten.

Royce, who made twice-weekly visits to The Del, depended upon associate manager Ernest Tiedemann and resident manager Alberto Campione to oversee day-to-day operations, both of whom became prominent presences at the hotel and throughout San Diego. During the summers, the Royce family — including red setter Timmy — lived at the Hotel Del, where Stephen Royce's involvement was more hands-on.

Another factor that figured into the hotel's survival during the Depression was its proximity to Hollywood, where, according to most historians, money was always available, some of it making its way down to The Del, which hosted a heyday of moviemaking and movie stars throughout the 1930s.

San Diego's military economy also buoyed The Del during the Depression, and after war was declared in Europe in 1939, the city received even more recruits (and their visiting families). By the time America entered the war in 1941, San Diego was a full-fledged "Navy town."

Continued on page 50

World War II Comes to The Del

With incoming Navy personnel, there was a housing crunch, especially in Coronado, where Naval Air Station North Island was churning out pilots. As a result, some Navy officers were housed at The Del in an allotment of rooms contracted by the Navy; however, thanks to Stephen Royce's advocacy, the hotel was able to remain a civilian resort throughout the war (many other American resorts were commandeered for the war effort, never to return to civilian use).

With Navy pilots in residence and North Island just down the road, The Del's World War II years were reportedly filled with a raucous social life. Stan Abele, a fighter pilot who went on to fly more than 40 combat missions and earned a Distinguished Flying Cross and three Air Medals, recalled, "The hotel was *the* party place — they had girls galore," affectionately calling his days at The Del "the best war I ever fought."

So prominent was the military during World War II that non-Navy guests were sometimes referred to as "the civilian set." William Singleton Davidson, a high school student during the war, remembers being awed by The Del's resident aviators: "The losses in some squadrons were 90 percent or more. They were the cream of American youth [and] a handsome lot ... [flying] in formation in groups of 20 or 30 ... directly over the hotel ... you could see their faces, and we would wave to them — sometimes they would dip their wings."

1920s Del Society

When "charming society girl" Rhoda Fullam married Raymond Welch in Coronado on Valentine's Day in 1920 (above), her extravagant nuptials featured an extensive bridal party, including Wallis Warfield Spencer (the future Duchess of Windsor) and her first husband, Lieutenant Commander Earl Winfield Spencer, Jr. (far right).

Rhoda's father was Rear Admiral William F. Fullam, and according to a lengthy newspaper account, most of the wedding guests were "members of the Navy set." The ceremony was held in a private home (and hence "comparatively small"); however, The Del's orchestra was called into service, where it played "the wedding marches," along with "soft music" during the ceremony.

In the 1920s, Coronado's social life revolved around the hotel, and Rhoda was described as a "social favorite," attending many galas, including a costume party (below right; Rhoda, Wallis Spencer and Rhoda's sister are standing, left to right).

Rhoda Fullam Welch continued to frequent The Del with her own children, Rhoda and Mariana, who formed a fashionable vignette in a hotel cabana in 1935 (below left). Sisters Rhoda and Mariana were also active in The Del's children's programs, and as a teenager, Rhoda was a member of the hotel's popular "Breakfast Club."

ABOVE AND TOP RIGHT
Two Hotel del Coronado buses were featured prominently in this c. 1920 promotional photo (above). A candid snapshot from the same period (right) advised guests: Autoists: Please do not open cut-outs on hotel grounds." Opening an automobile's cut-out valve resulted in increased power, but it circumvented the muffler and created more noise.

MIDDLE RIGHT
A group of Sunday sailors posed in a beached rowboat, c. 1920.

BOTTOM RIGHT
In 1922, Ruben and Minnie Finkelstein honeymooned in San Diego and had their photos taken at the hotel; 63 years later, their granddaughter married at The Del.

CORONADO BEACH.

ON an exquisite necklace of sand which separates San Diego Bay from the ocean, is Coronado, a jewel-city of prosperous homes, from the bungalow type to the pretentious mansion, with fine streets and beautiful parks, and is a center for out-of-door recreation activities on land and water. ❧ One of its chief attractions is the world famous Hotel del Coronado, one of the largest and best known of resort hotels. The hotel faces the beach, and is surrounded by lawns, flowers and tropical verdure. The hotel itself is always gay with its winter and summer colonies and their social activities. Coronado is the original home of midwinter Polo. ❧ Another feature of special interest is Tent City, in summertime, with its several thousand inhabitants, who live but a minute distant from the soft ocean surges on one side, and the placid Bay on the other. ❧ The new and fascinating sport of aquaplaning and its accompaniments of swimming, yachting, motor-boating, launch parties, beach picnics, clam bakes and water carnivals, make time fly. ❧ Nearby are polo fields, golf links and tennis courts. ❧ Near Coronado Beach are innumerable places of interest. The Naval Air Station and Rockwell Aviation Field at North Island are but fifteen minutes by auto. Across the Bay, are attractions of San Diego including Ramona's Marriage Place, Mission Cliff Gardens, Balboa Park, Point Loma, Theosophical Institute, Marine Base Naval Training Station, Sunset Cliffs, Mission Beach, the enchanted cliffs and caves of La Jolla, and Old Mexico with its quaint customs and interesting sights.

TOP LEFT
A booklet of postcards c. 1931 included a wonderful depiction of the hotel, along with an overview of the resort's amenities and attractions.

BOTTOM LEFT
The Del's stationery in 1937.

TOP RIGHT
The hotel's bell staff in 1932.

BOTTOM RIGHT
Promotional photos graced the interior of a hotel envelope in 1938. Although the total number of adult guests decreased during the Depression (and by the mid-1930s, child guests were almost nonexistent), the number of visitors who traveled with servants remained strong, running as high as one servant for every 15 adult guests (in 1936). Still, daily average room revenue between 1929 and 1938 dropped from approximately $15.15 to $10.24.

How Stephen Royce Saved The Del

Hotel manager Stephen Royce — who hailed from a family of wealthy hoteliers — saw The Del through the tough days of the Depression and World War II. Brought in to help the Depression-strapped Del turn a profit, Royce succeeded with a series of structural and social additions.

At the beginning of his tenure (1934–1948), Royce oversaw a "gigantic remodeling campaign," which included the addition of tennis courts, swimming pool and cabanas, as well as the establishment of the "Beach & Tennis Club" ("a deluxe club"), all designed to entice Royce's well-to-do Pasadena and San Francisco social circles south. Elaborate pool parties and other pool-related functions soon followed — from fashion shows to high-diving exhibitions.

The Royce family was so well connected socially that when Stephen offered his Pasadena-based wife the opportunity for their teenage daughter, Dorothy, to be First Lady Eleanor Roosevelt's swimming companion during Roosevelt's 1935 visit (Mrs. Roosevelt had been advised against swimming alone), Mrs. Royce was not even tempted. According to Royce's son, Danny, his mother's reaction was something along the lines of "Have you gone nuts? I'm not about to spend four hours driving Dorothy down to go swimming with Mrs. Roosevelt!" (At that time, the only route between Pasadena and Coronado was on the coast road; there were no freeways to speed the trip.)

With Royce's society connections, he was able to institute yachting regattas at The Del, with the hotel hosting "most of the social affairs," including reception parties, dinner dances and award ceremonies. He expanded The Del's boathouse, adding wide verandas from which to view the bay races, which often featured San Francisco–based yachts. Ocean races were viewed from the hotel, which offered "an unsurpassed view of the roads."

Royce also created the "Rainbow Fleet," a collection of matching boats with colorful sails (featured prominently in hotel promotional materials), providing endless entertainment for children and adults. Aquaplaning also became popular during his reign. In addition, Royce instituted everything from bridge-playing contests to theatrical performances and started The Del's retail department, renting space to local merchants. In 1938, he oversaw the hotel's 50th birthday celebration. Thanks to Royce, The Del enjoyed a socially rich era despite the Depression, with San Diego newspapers following the activities of hotel debutantes, whom they referred to as "debbies."

At about the same time — when, according to son Danny, nearby "servicemen were looking for something to do" — Royce converted a storage area into the hotel's famed Circus Room, which became a popular San Diego watering hole. With few refurbishing supplies available at the time, Royce initially used Ringling Brothers' circus posters to decorate the walls.

Royce can also be credited with single-handedly talking the military out of taking over The Del during World War II. Taking the bull by the horns, Royce contacted local military officials in 1943, and according to a transcribed telephone conversation, he implored the Navy to preserve The Del as a civilian resort:

We have always tried to give priority to families of the men who are here because we think that maybe it will be the last time they will see them ... and this way the hotel is recreation, with other guests coming and going and friends; it is relaxation as well as a place to live.

For its part, the Navy agreed: "The hotel is serving a very definite need for recreation and welfare of not only the officers that live in the hotel but we have a large colony [of Navy] in Coronado."

After the war, Royce oversaw another decade milestone, The Del's 60th birthday in 1948, before relocating to Hawaii to manage his family's other hotels.

ABOVE

During summers, manager Stephen Royce and his family lived at The Del. A variety of photos from son Danny's scrapbook illustrates the children's active social life — sailing, as a member of the Rainbow Fleet; dog Timmy in the courtyard; a poolside parade; a meeting of the "Breakfast Club"; and gathered with friends in the Garden Patio.

1888 1938 GOLDEN JUBILEE HOTEL del CORONADO

THIS PAGE
The hotel's 50th birthday celebration in 1938 included a ceremonial train ride for guests attired in period costumes. The occasion also brought forth a short construction history by architect James Reid, who wrote, "Whatever merit there is, goes to Messrs. Babcock and Story ... who built greater than they knew."

The Fortnighter *Chronicles* Guest Activities: 1938–1949

The Hotel del Coronado's newsletter, *The Fortnighter*, kept guests up-to-date on hotel happenings throughout the '30s and '40s.

1930s

According to newsletters, even as late as the 1930s, some hotel guests still followed the Victorian pattern of wintering at The Del for the entire season. Resident guests — those who lived full time at The Del — had their "vacations" elsewhere reported in *The Fortnighter.*

With the Spreckels family holding the reins until 1948, their family's news received wide play, with one 1939 issue reporting, "Tiny Lois Spreckels is making the big folks sit up and take notice of her swimming prowess. She cuts the water like a fish."

1940s

In 1942, there was a reference to Mr. and Mrs. W.E. Boeing, who were "simply delighted with their rooms on the oceanfront. Besides his interest in the big Boeing factories, Mr. Boeing's hobby — and what a lovely one, too — is race horses."

The newsletters also included guest updates from afar, with a 1942 issue featuring a poetic contribution from New Hampshire: "So revel in memories of frolics and rides; your pool and your rooms, where pleasure abides!"

The February 1942 newsletter — on the heels of the Pearl Harbor attack — was replete with military references, including updates about "defense stamps" ("remember that each little stamp packs a terrific wallop for liberty and democracy"); hotel-based Red Cross fundraising and knitting ("the championship being conceded to Mrs. A.C. Smith … she does the most difficult helmets and the big sea-boots, which are her special assignment because of her excellent work"); and the American Women's Volunteer Services (AWVS): "Many of the women guests give a part of each day to making bandages and surgical dressings in the bridge room, which has been turned over to the AWVS."

A 1948 issue was noteworthy for its references to the hotel's upcoming 60th birthday celebration, along with a photo of Bette Davis with the caption "'What's for dinner?' smilingly asks Bette Davis of her husband, William Grant Sherry." California Governor Earl Warren — later the 14th Chief Justice of the United States — also made an appearance at The Del that month, where he was described as looking "quite chipper."

In the August 1948 issue, screen star George Murphy, his wife and their "moppets" were featured. Other photos highlighted a Hawaiian poolside luau, returning summer guests and the latest in a steady stream of Del honeymooners, referred to as "the celebrated Hotel del Coronado fraternity of Matrimonial Matriculators."

Pauline Friedman: Resident Guest

In 1938, Pauline Friedman became a resident guest, along with her parents, who kept separate accommodations. At that time, the Friedmans were part of a population that included about 100 resident guests (it would dwindle to a couple dozen by the 1950s).

In a magazine article, Friedman, who was born in 1910, was described as "extremely attractive, a stylish adventurer and enthusiastic athlete, excelling at golf, swimming, tennis and riding. She led a cultured life, socializing and traveling the world … pampered and indulged all her life."

During her residence at The Del, Friedman "never had any responsibilities": She entertained friends in the cocktail lounge, had her laundry done on site, and took all her meals in the hotel. For an extra fee, Friedman was allowed to keep a small dog in her room, whose meals of fresh chopped meat were provided by Room Service. According to Friedman's memoir, she enjoyed one of the longest guest tenures, moving out after a stay of almost 40 years.

ABOVE
Pauline Friedman in the Garden Patio with her dog Thrifty; Pauline's father relaxing on The Del's porch; Pauline and her brother Julius, poolside, all circa 1940.

World War II Remembered

Marine Pilot

Warren Goodman, a World War II Marine pilot who was housed at the Hotel del Coronado in 1942–43, recalled:

The Hotel del Coronado contributed to the war effort by providing housing for officers during World War II. Many hotels in the country boast of having participated in the war effort, but almost all of them were taken over by the military and went out of business for the duration. The Del was unusual because it was doing its regular business while devoting some rooms to officer housing. That, and the fact that the officers were treated as regular guests, instead of being segregated in a portion of the hotel, was what made my stay so enjoyable and contributed greatly to my morale at that time.

The retired lieutenant colonel recounted additional memories in a Reserve Officers' Association newsletter:

The hotel was about ten minutes from the Naval Air Station, but there was a free bus running between the two. Thus, it was convenient to get to the base for meals and musters or to use the pool, officers' club or tennis courts. But you could also opt to use the hotel pool, beach and tennis courts free of charge. You could also use the hotel bar, have meals in the opulent dining room or even call for Room Service and run a tab payable weekly.

A Happy Military Misunderstanding

Another happy World War II memory came from Dorabel Crook, who was married to a captain in the Army Air Corps. In 1943, when the young couple made reservations at The Del to rendezvous with her Navy brother-in-law, the hotel assumed that "Captain" Crook was a Navy captain (a high rank in the Navy; a much lower rank in the Army). As Dorabel remembers:

So we went to Coronado and checked into the hotel. We were shown to our room. As soon as the door was opened, our mouths flew open, and my husband said surely there was a mistake. The room had doors opening to a balcony with an ocean view and white wicker furniture with a chaise lounge. It was assumed that Captain Crook was a Navy captain, and in 1943, Navy captains were few and far between [stateside]. We were too green to know the difference.

European Royalty

More than one World War II–era guest remembers that the hotel became a haven for displaced members of European royalty, forced from their homelands as ancient monarchies tumbled; they added an international and old-world cachet to The Del. As longtime guest Bettie Magee recalled:

From about 1939 on, another glamorous group lived at the hotel. These were the displaced nobility of occupied countries in Europe. Most of them were elderly, but there were some who were young and possibly in line for a European throne.

Their clothes were beautiful, unusual and old-fashioned, and the women wore gleaming jewels — necklaces, bracelets and earrings. Even I could tell they were real gems. We called one couple "the Baron and Baroness."

Del Wartime Novel

In the novel *Madmen Must*, William Jovanovich, future president of Harcourt Brace Jovanovich, detailed his days as a hotel waiter in 1941, after which he joined the Navy before launching his meteoric publishing career. Set almost entirely at The Del, the 1978 book focuses on the day-to-day life of a young college graduate who heads west to wait tables.

Among other things, Jovanovich talked about the hotel's employee dormitory, mentioned his weekly paycheck ($33.20), described his uniform ("a red Philip Morris jacket with an elastic loop holding its two wings together") and explained how Room Service waiters could jockey for bigger tips: "You could find out about arriving guests by bribing one of the desk clerks; you could also keep an eye on the florist shop, where large bouquets were being made ready for notable guests."

After his year at The Del, Jovanovich was stationed at North Island and served in the Navy from 1942 to 1946.

ABOVE
Bettie Morris Magee with her father, Benjamin Morris, on the front steps of the hotel in 1943.

TOP LEFT
A Hotel Del guest recently identified two of these women from a 1942 photo as her mother Maureen Moriarty and friend Helen Abbott, both of whom were widowed by the war.

TOP RIGHT
A World War II–era postcard.

BOTTOM RIGHT AND ABOVE
Melody Hyde Morgan, a Coronado native whose family belonged to the Beach & Tennis Club, posed for a Del publicity photo and also served as a volunteer in the hotel's American Women's Volunteer Services program (above photo, in the back row, far left), c. 1943.

ROOM SERVICE DISCONTINUED
EFFECTIVE SUNDAY, MAY 23, 1943

Due to the acute shortage of manpower, it is necessary for us to discontinue Room Service.

We regret any inconvenience to our guests but trust that you will understand the circumstances.

THE MANAGEMENT
HOTEL DEL CORONADO

Dining-Room hours are as follows:

Breakfast   7 to 9:30
Luncheon   12:30 to 1:45
Dinner   6:30 to 8:00

THIS PAGE ABOVE AND TOP LEFT
Allan Christie, a British Navy officer from New Zealand, who was "billeted" at The Del in 1943 during his training at North Island, later remembered, "You can visualize our looks of amazement when we arrived at the Del Coronado." Other memories included his New Zealand roommate meeting his future wife at the hotel, and actor Gary Cooper playing a lot of "patience" (solitaire). Christie enjoyed the beach (above) and donned heavy flight gear for a photo with his fellow New Zealand officers (above left), for which the former lieutenant (standing, second from left) apologized: "Our leather jackets were for the photographer's benefit and do not imply that Coronado weather was too cold."

THIS PAGE BOTTOM
The hotel announced the end of Room Service in 1943.

THIS PAGE MIDDLE
Navy pilot Fred Swearingen, housed at The Del in 1944, is shown here in the Circus Room (second man from right).

FACING PAGE TOP RIGHT AND TOP LEFT
Lisle West's c. 1944 aircraft carrier "memory book" included pages of Del photos. Pilots such as West remembered The Del as a wonderful refuge from intense training and what lay ahead.

FACING PAGE BOTTOM RIGHT
A guest bill from 1945 illustrates the special $2 military room rates.

FACING PAGE BOTTOM LEFT
The country's patriotism was reflected in this 1945 table setting.

Jes' Pals

DEL CORONADO NITES

Thas where my money Goes!

CORONADO · **HOTEL DEL CORONADO** · CALIFORNIA				A 40977		
LEE, LT. WALTER 2221 BROAD AVE. ALTOONA, PENNSYLVANIA	Guests Arrived	1 11/29	FP	WEDNESDAY		
	Rate					
	Rooms	2.00		Reg. No.		
Memo	Date	Explanation		Amount Charged	Amount Credited	Balance Due
1	AUG-8-45	FWARD		★ 17.96		★ 17.96
2	AUG-8-45	LNDRY		★ 1.54		★ 19.50
3	AUG-8-45	ROOM ●● ●●		★ 2.00		
4	AUG-8-45	PHONE ●● ●●		★ 0.10		★ 21.60
5	AUG-9-45	MEALS		★ 4.10		25.70
6	AUG-9-45	ROOM ●●		★ 2.00		★ 27.70
7	AUG10-45	MEALS		★ 4.10		★ 31.80
8	AUG10-45	ROOM ●● ●●		★ 2.00		★ 33.80
9	AUG11-45	ROOM ●● ●●		★ 2.00		★ 35.80
10	AUG12-45	PAID			★ 38.00	★ 2.20 CR
11	AUG12-45	ROOM ●● ●●		★ 2.00		
12	AUG12-45	PHONE ●● ●●		★ 0.20		★ 0.00 CR
13	AUG13-45	PHONE		★ 0.20		★ 0.20
14						
15						
16						
17						
18						
19						
20						
21						
22						
23						
24						

HOTEL del CORONADO PAID AUG 13 1945

BILLS ARE DUE WHEN RENDERED

First day's charge for board and room carries account from actual time of arrival until after breakfast the following morning

Last Amount in This Column is Balance Due

Lee

THIS PAGE
With the war over, The Del produced some new
promotional photos.

TOP RIGHT AND ABOVE

Doris Skinner Treadwell, who vacationed at The Del for 20 years, penned a lengthy poem about the hotel in honor of its 60th birthday celebration (top right), which read, in part:

> And Coronado by the sea
> Welcomed a grown-up girl in me.
> A big pine tree near the dining room
> Old Santa did with lights festoon.
> And, oh, how good it was to dine
> In that lovely long room at Christmas time.

Treadwell, along with her granddaughter, was also featured in a 1948 guest newsletter (above).

BOTTOM RIGHT

In 1948, the hotel celebrated its 60th birthday.

Postwar Mobility

After World War II, Americans were on the move, with the Hotel del Coronado transitioning from a "railroad resort" to a destination connected by an ever-expanding highway system. This increased mobility was a challenge for establishments like The Del, with many vacationers preferring to go where they hadn't gone before, often choosing modern motels (a shortened version of "motor hotels") over prewar destinations.

No doubt The Del suffered from the nation's growing affection for highway-accessible accommodations, where postwar travelers often spent just one night (not their entire vacations) and could park their automobiles right out front — both a convenience and a display of affluence. In 1958, the country's first Holiday Inn in Memphis, Tennessee, spoke to the 1950s mindset: It offered drive-through check-in, the height of luxury and sophistication for many of America's vacationers, a population that continued to grow by leaps and bounds.

1950s

While The Del might not have been as appealing to some as a drive-through Holiday Inn, it was still a popular postwar destination, helped along by a legion of faithful followers, many of whom were generational guests, connected to the hotel by family members who had come before.

Under Barney Goodman's ownership (1948–1960), the wealthy "colony" from Kansas City (Goodman's residence) expanded. Another contingent was drawn from Oklahoma, where the oil business was booming.

In tribute to its continuing popularity with Hollywood folks, a July 27, 1950, hotel newsletter was awash with references of celebrity visitors, including Hume Cronyn and Jessica Tandy, Mr. and Mrs. William Powell, Lucille Ball and Desi Arnaz, Liberace, and Rosalind Russell and husband. The next year, the newsletter featured a photo of FDR's son James Roosevelt and family (from Beverly Hills), along with references of visits by celebs Groucho and Harpo Marx, Loretta Young, Errol Flynn and wife Patricia Wymore, and entertainer Hildegarde.

Continued on page 64

RIGHT
The nation's postwar optimism was reflected in the hotel's colorful letterhead artwork.

Throughout the 1950s, The Del's Beach & Tennis Club was in full swing, with many Coronado families renting poolside cabanas for the entire summer. Some even had indefinite leases, and before long these temporary tents began to take on the look of permanent retreats, complete with wooden walls and personal furnishings, becoming status symbols for the most-established tenants. This was a heyday for Coronado's youth, who enjoyed The Del as their own private playground, participating in pool activities, tennis matches and a myriad of social events. In fact, it would be a rare 1950s Coronado kid who wasn't completely familiar with the hotel's complicated hallways — and as one Coronadan remembers, "We all knew how to get out on the roof."

Some Like It Hot

While the summer seasons boomed, the hotel's business dipped once school was back in session, but this laidback lull may have worked in The Del's favor, prompting director Billy Wilder to film his classic movie, *Some Like It Hot*, along the beach in September 1958 (see pages 182–187).

Wilder liked the fact that the Hotel Del could pass as a 1920s resort, which suited the storyline of the film. With the crowds thinned, Wilder and his film crew (numbering around 100) probably had the run of the resort, not counting the hundreds of day trippers who came over from San Diego, trying to catch sight of Marilyn Monroe and other stars.

1963: A Snapshot in Time

A 1963 "Information and Service Directory" provided comprehensive and detailed information about life at The Del during the 1960s, featuring a few dozen alphabetized entries, including the following:

Arcade Shops: Enjoy shopping in the Arcade on the terrace level: Women's Fashions, Haberdashery, Jewels, Children's Modes, Barber Shop ("complete barbering service, manicurist and shine boy"), Beauty Salon, Photographic Studio, Flower Shop ("Crown House Too"), Television and Radio Shop.

Beach & Tennis Club: Complete facilities are available at no extra charge to guests of the hotel. Cabanas may be reserved and rented by the day, week or month. The Turquoise Pool's filtered saltwater is heated. Four championship tennis courts; equipment and instruction available.

Candy Cane Playground: Our specially equipped children's amusement center is constructed on a base of fine sand. A trained instructor schedules and supervises activities — permitting greater freedom and enjoyment both for parents and the youngsters.

Chiropodist and Podiatrist: Office on the terrace level.

Cocktails: Casino Lounge; Victorian Lounge ("enjoy the rich-hued elegance of turn-of-the-century décor with your favorite aperitifs of liqueurs"); Ocean View Room (an "indoor-outdoor lounge"); and Luau Room ("Among the exotic decorations in this popular lounge, you'll discover a miniature waterfall — and surely a tiki to tickle your fancy. Potions with Polynesian personality or customary cocktail fare").

Dancing and Entertainment: Year-round in the Ocean View Room on weekends.

Dining: Crown Room ("Sorry — no beach attire permitted; please wear coat and tie for evening dining"); Luau Room ("delicious Cantonese dinners"); and Coffee Shop ("a bright and charming choice for informal dining, tasty snacks and fountain treats").

Notary Public: Contact Public Stenographer on lobby level.

Pitch-and-Putt Course: On the hotel grounds.

Pressing: Call Bell Captain; refer also to "Laundry" listing.

Reservations: When you are in Los Angeles, contact our office in the Biltmore Hotel.

A promotional mailing for 1963 — The Del's 75th anniversary — provided additional information about the summer season. The hotel was now on the European plan (no longer were meals included in the price of guestrooms); room rates were listed simply: single rooms from $12; double rooms from $15.

Here Comes the Bridge

One of the most noteworthy turning points in Hotel Del history occurred in 1964, when the decision was made to build a bay bridge, connecting Coronado to San Diego (see pages 72–75). While John D. Spreckels had had a similar idea in 1926, it was scuttled by the Army Corps of Engineers. Later proposals were usually thwarted by the U.S. Navy, which was afraid a bridge would impede ship traffic (the idea of a drawbridge — Spreckels' original concept — was considered completely unworkable).

A 1928 guest letter addressed the hotel's sometimes inconvenient location with regard to San Diego ... and even referenced Spreckels' bridge proposal:

If there was only some way of getting the crowd over to San Diego without having to drive around the Strand, the hotel would go like wildfire. There was some talk of building a bridge across, but the Navy put a crimp in that. They don't want any interference for their ships.

It wasn't until decades later, after the California State Division of Highways got involved, that the Pentagon agreed to a bridge, with groundbreaking in 1967. Two years later, the San Diego–Coronado Bay Bridge was complete, with its soaring arc design well above the tallest Navy ship and its elongated silhouette allowing for the gradual inclines necessary for automobile traffic.

After the bridge, life in Coronado changed, as its pace and population gradually increased. The Del, in turn, became a more desirable destination, connected to the San Diego airport and sightseeing by a speedy trip across the bridge.

This replaced the time-consuming ferries (although the ride itself was brief, loading and unloading cars was not). During rush hour, the ferries could not keep pace with the commuters, who were often backed up for blocks along Orange Avenue.

THIS PAGE
A c. 1955 brochure (right) included a photo of a guestroom (above).

"What's more fun than swinging?" say Katharine and Frances Tucker, daughters of Mrs. James Tucker of Piedmont.

Tennis is always "big time" at Coronado. Finalists in the weekly Round Robin tournament were Max Hayman, Los Angeles; Helen Lauinger, Tulsa; Bob Rogaff and Richie Zall, Beverly Hills.

The P.C. Lauingers of Tulsa need no introduction! Among Coronado's "favorite families," they're tops. With Mrs. Frank Lauinger and Mr. and Mrs. P.C. Lauinger are Frank, Mary, Philip and Helen. On the mats are Tony, Fran and Joe.

A golden wedding anniversary. Celebrants are Mr. and Mrs. Sam Logan of Toledo.

You're right. That's the well-known Roosevelt smile. Mr. and Mrs. James Roosevelt with James, Jr., Michael and Nell. Their home is in Beverly Hills.

Three generations of the Soden family, of Kansas City, have kept Hotel del Coronado young and gay. Among this summer's visitors were Mrs. Robert Soden, Jack, Steve and Robert Soden, Michael Mayer, Mickey Zahner, Mrs. John W. Soden, Sandy Mayer and Mrs. Mayer.

Sailing picnic held top fun priority this summer. Some San Francisco fans included Mr. and Mrs. Frederick Coleman, Stevie and Freddie Coleman, Wally Marks, Nancy Vaughn and Renee Altura.

Three wonderful ladies–and three wonderful names in the hotel world! Mrs. E. M. Statler of New York, Mrs. James McCabe of Los Angeles and Mrs. Carl Stanley of Carmel. Hope you visit us again–real soon.

THIS PAGE AND FACING PAGE
Guest photos were the order of the day throughout the 1950s, when the hotel employed a resident photographer. These pictures were featured in guest newsletters in 1951 and 1953 (captions are original) and reflect the hotel's varied clientele, which included older, traditional folks as well as more-modern, younger guests.

Mr. and Mrs. J.A. Morrison holidayed here from Los Angeles. Oh yes, Susie is the party of the third part.

Hotel employees posed for a group photo in 1954. Seated, left to right: Marion Davidson, social director; Ted Hradsky, office manager; Ernest Tiedemann, resident manager; Ashton Stanley, managing director; Alfred Hansen, executive assistant manager, John Tetley, sales manager; Nelle Thomas, executive housekeeper. Standing, left to right: Charles Swafford, director of advertising; Gayne Kinsey, manager of Beach & Tennis Club; Seren Kassapian, director of publicity; Jack Fletcher, manager of bars; Edward Gillette, food and beverage controller; William Schwarz, catering manager; D.M. Eastman, executive chef; Eugene Logan, chief accountant; John Tiedemann, chief steward; Thomas Walsh, assistant catering manager; Nora Cartter, chief telephone operator; Alfred Laing, manager of laundry; Eddie Bergman, musical director; G.W. Huntridge, superintendant of maintenance.

TOP LEFT
Thanks to the benign neglect the hotel endured during the Depression and World War II, the front façade had not yet been modernized when this 1953 postcard was produced, one of the reasons director Billy Wilder chose The Del for his Some Like It Hot *setting. The imprint on the reverse side of the postcard read: "The Hotel del Coronado is one of the few old-time famous luxury hotels left in the country."*

BOTTOM LEFT
A Del wedding, c. 1958.

TOP RIGHT
A publicity photo, c. 1958.

BOTTOM RIGHT
Owner Barney Goodman's daughter, with husband and children, in the Garden Patio, c. 1958.

FACING PAGE
By 1960, a porte cochere had been added to the hotel.

THIS PAGE TOP LEFT AND TOP RIGHT
Distinctive 1960-era artwork illustrated the 1963 "Information and Service Directory."

THIS PAGE BOTTOM LEFT
The hotel unveiled a new telephone switchboard, c. 1961.

THIS PAGE BOTTOM RIGHT
An April 1963 guest newsletter, Hotel del Coronado Notes, *featured John Provost with his television costar Lassie, who "completely enthralled children at the Hotel del Coronado as they mingled comfortably with youthful guests during Easter Week activities." The newsletter also included photos of Lana Turner and the Lennon sisters.*

The Coronado Bridge

The spectacular San Diego–Coronado Bay Bridge — a sculptural span of architectural splendor — is a masterpiece of design. More than 2 miles in length, with a visually dramatic 90-degree shift at midpoint, this elegant stretch is supported by equally elegant arches, reminiscent of the graceful design found in California's early missions.

Constructed of concrete and steel, the structure is described as "orthotropic," which means that the arches hide all the supporting struts and braces, giving the bridge an artful silhouette. The bridge's color — a beautiful shade of sparkling blue — speaks to Southern California's year-round sunny skies and is one of the most-photographed images in San Diego.

Views from the bridge are commanding and unobstructed (the side panels are only 34 inches high). Coming into Coronado, one can see the Hotel del Coronado and the Pacific Ocean (sunsets are spectacular), as well as the bayfront golf course.

The bridge makes it quick and easy to travel into San Diego, but the expanse of bay helps maintain Coronado as an island-like paradise, a "world away" from the hustle and bustle of the big city.

Although San Diego is visually close — Coronado boasts the most-photographed view of the city's famous bayfront skyline — the city was not readily accessible until the bridge was completed. In the early days, traveling up the Strand — originally by train or horse, eventually by car — was the only way to reach Coronado via land. This time-consuming, roundabout route explains the popularity of the hotel's original ferry system, which transported guests, along with their horses and buggies (and eventually their cars), across the bay.

Today, a picturesque pedestrian ferry is in service between Coronado's bayfront dock and downtown San Diego; the breezy, beautiful trip takes about 10 minutes.

THIS PAGE ABOVE
The 1969 San Diego–Coronado Bay Bridge during construction, along with a rendering of John D. Spreckels' 1926 proposal.

FACING PAGE TOP
This photo was taken during one of the car ferry's last runs. After the bridge was opened in 1969, the ferry system was shut down (replaced by a pedestrian ferry some years later).

FACING PAGE BOTTOM
Opening day ceremonies on August 2, 1969, included a parade of vintage cars coming into Coronado (left), after which the first motorists to use the bridge were photographed (right).

A New Day Dawns at The Del

With the Coronado Bridge in place, The Del was able to step forward as a hospitality leader, a necessity for its long-term survival. As recently as the early 1960s, the hotel's future had been uncertain: It was decidedly past its prime, and it was being passed by as vacationers and conventioneers alike sought San Diego's more-contemporary facilities. So dire was The Del's situation that there was talk of razing the hotel.

Fortunately, the convenience of the Coronado Bridge made all the difference, and the hotel began adding to its inventory of guestrooms and meeting space, a competitive necessity. Today, The Del is in an ideal position to meet the demands of vacation travelers (who peak in the summer and during holidays) and meeting travelers (who fill the slower in-between times).

Toward a Centennial Celebration

During the '70s, '80s and most of the '90s, the hotel was owned by M. Larry Lawrence. As with every Hotel Del owner who preceded him, Lawrence had personal wealth and the desire to put The Del on the map. With Lawrence at the helm, the hotel was modernized, becoming a solidly popular and profitable resort. He added approximately 300 guestrooms with the construction of Ocean Towers in 1973 and California Cabanas in 1979. Grande Hall, a state-of-the-art meeting and banquet facility, was opened in 1973.

In the 1980s, enhancement efforts were helped along by America's booming economy. During this period, The Del's distinctive Ballroom turret became an advertising icon, incorporated into its logo (the earliest logos featured crowns).

Heritage Tourism and the Hotel Del

Contributing to The Del's success in the second half of the 20th century was the nation's 1976 bicentennial, which inspired citizens — well in advance of the celebration itself — to look at "old" in a new way. Increasingly intrigued by both history and historic preservation,

Continued on page 76

RIGHT
After the completion of the Coronado Bridge in 1969, the Hotel Del frequently included it in its promotion. The imprinted text on the reverse side of this postcard reads: "In this exceptional aerial view, the nineteenth-century elegance of the magnificent Hotel del Coronado contrasts beautifully with the modern grace of the San Diego–Coronado Bay Bridge."

vacationers sought historic hotels for the one-of-a-kind experiences they provided, and the concept of heritage tourism began to emerge.

In 1977 — after years of painstaking effort and documentation — the Hotel del Coronado was designated a National Historic Landmark by the National Trust for Historic Preservation. This was followed by additional preservation accomplishments when two Coronado buildings destined for destruction were moved to hotel property and retrofitted for contemporary use: the Oxford Building in 1987 and the Windsor Cottage in 1989.

The 1887 Oxford Building — Coronado's first hotel — was moved to Del property and restored in 1987. Before the Hotel Del opened in 1888, the Oxford housed Del management; later it was purchased by the hotel, serving as a dormitory for employees. After The Del's ownership ended, the Oxford fell into disrepair until the hotel intervened in its restoration.

The Windsor Cottage — one of the Coronado homes Wallis Simpson (later the Duchess of Windsor) lived in during the 1920s — was going to be replaced with a newer home. Today, this c. 1905 California beach bungalow is an ocean-side reception/social area for Beach Village guests and Club at The Del members.

In 1988, the Hotel del Coronado celebrated its 100th birthday. The centennial party was filled with Hollywood celebrities and included a variety of commemorative events, including a polo match on the beach.

The One and Only Del

Today, the Hotel del Coronado is a Southern California landmark and continues to reign supreme as the premier resort on the Pacific coast.

An extensive restoration and preservation effort begun in 1999 ensured The Del well into the next century. As the centerpiece of the resort's ocean-side façade, Windsor Lawn — an expanse of Victorian lawn, walkways and award-winning gardens — was created, reestablishing The Del's connection to the beach. Complementing Windsor Lawn, seaside restaurants, bars and shops were added, which included the meticulous restoration of the hotel's original 46-foot mahogany bar. Air-conditioning was installed in all Victorian Building guestrooms; the Crown Room's roof was raised and retrofitted; and a variety of other structural and aesthetic enhancements were made.

In 2007, The Del unveiled Beach Village, an enclave of 78 luxury beachside accommodations that feature living/dining areas as well as kitchens, fireplaces, balconies and terraces.

The Del's culinary department continues to distinguish itself. Its signature restaurant, 1500 OCEAN, serves up spectacular sunsets along with Southland coastal cuisine, for which the hotel's vegetable and herb garden provides just-picked produce. There is also Sunday brunch in the Crown Room (consistently voted "Best in San Diego"), which also hosts holiday celebrations for Thanksgiving, Christmas, New Year's, Easter and Mother's Day.

The Del's retail department — conceived during the depths of the Depression — is now a bustling collection of more than 17 shops, offering Del keepsakes and collectibles, resort wear, jewelry, home fashions, children's toys and more.

Spa at The Del is among the newer additions, with 21 treatment rooms and an ocean-view vanishing-edge pool, along with a state-of-the-art fitness center.

Resort activities are more diverse than ever, offering everything from surfing classes (unheard of for most 19th-century guests) to ice-skating on the beach (something Victorians enjoyed — though never in Southern California).

Future History

The history of the Hotel del Coronado is always ongoing.

When Elisha Babcock and Hampton Story conceived The Del in 1885, they envisioned a resort where "people will continue to come long after we are gone." Since then, both fortune and fate have determined the hotel's history. Today — thanks to dedicated and visionary stewardship — The Del is poised to reign for another 100 years.

FACING PAGE TOP LEFT
A c. 1973 brochure was still promoting the 1969 completion of the Coronado Bridge.

FACING PAGE BOTTOM LEFT
The National Park Service designated the Hotel del Coronado a National Historic Landmark in 1977.

FACING PAGE TOP RIGHT
Ocean Towers and Grande Hall were both unveiled in 1973 (top two drawings). Ocean Towers offered an additional 200 guestrooms to the hotel's inventory; Grande Hall was equipped for large group functions. In 1979, the 100-room California Cabanas were added (bottom drawing); the building also included function rooms.

FACING PAGE BOTTOM RIGHT
A more modern take on the hotel's logo (c. 1979) reflected the resort's increasingly contemporary image.

Now easy to get to by
the San Diego-Coronado Bay Bridge...
America's world-renowned
ocean-front resort

Hotel
del Coronado

Coronado, California

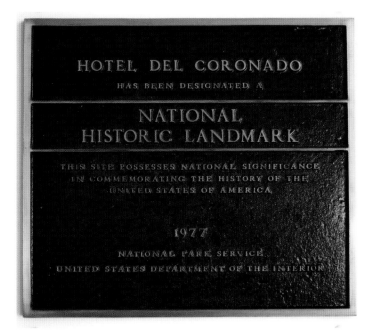

World-renowned

Hotel del Coronado

1500 Orange Ave., Coronado, Ca. 92118 (619) 435-6611

LEFT
A 1981 hotel brochure captured the endless recreational possibilities at The Del.

ABOVE
Already gearing up for its 1988 centennial, the hotel celebrated its 95th birthday in 1983 with a party in the Garden Patio.

ABOVE
This 1984 promotional piece captures a snapshot in time, when California's summer was packed with the Democratic Convention in San Francisco and the Olympics in Los Angeles. By comparison, The Del remained "uncrowded, enjoyable."

TOP RIGHT
As illustrated in this 1982 brochure, The Del's turret logo is ever-evolving.

BOTTOM RIGHT
Junior Miss America finalists posed with the hotel's sign in 1987.

THE UNITED STATES POSTAL SERVICE
PROUDLY COMMEMORATES
THE 100th ANNIVERSARY OF THE
HOTEL del CORONADO

THIS PAGE
In 1988, the Hotel del Coronado celebrated its centennial birthday with an elaborate banquet in the Crown Room (top left) and a display of hot-air balloons (top right) — a nod to the fact that hot-air balloons had been used in the promotion of the hotel's construction. The hotel also unveiled a new logo (bottom right), and the United States Postal Service honored The Del with a special cancellation in Coronado (bottom left).

LEFT

In 1997, a photographer captured Grande Hall's bank of pay phones, which were located in a warmly decorated and beautifully lighted area, with privacy screens between. This was a promotional plus in the pre–cell phone era, when busy conventioneers needed a convenient and comfortable way to keep in contact with their business responsibilities back home.

ABOVE

American resorts tell the history of our times, as this photo illustrates. In 1990, at the conclusion of Desert Storm, the Hotel Del honored returning servicemembers with a large yellow ribbon atop its famous turret (yellow ribbons had become a universally recognized symbol of support).

Once in a blue moon, comes a hotel beyond compare.

World-Renowned
HOTEL
DEL
CORONADO
A National Historic Landmark
Celebrating A Lifelong Romance With The Pacific

CORONADO, CALIFORNIA
A NATIONAL HISTORIC LANDMARK

World-Renowned
HOTEL
DEL
CORONADO®

Celebrating A Lifelong Romance With The Pacific.

RIGHT AND TOP LEFT
*In the 1990s, the "world-renowned Hotel del Coronado"
included the tagline "Celebrating A Lifelong Romance With
The Pacific" (right), which was later expanded with a reference
to its National Historic Landmark status (top).*

BOTTOM LEFT
*What's wrong with this picture? The Del's sprawling
architecture is sometimes hard to keep track of, as shown in
this c. 1990 photo, where the turret is to the left of the hotel's
beachside façade instead of to its right. Although the staff did
not catch the mistake until after the photo was printed in a
brochure, it's likely many hotel guests wouldn't have noticed
the error.*

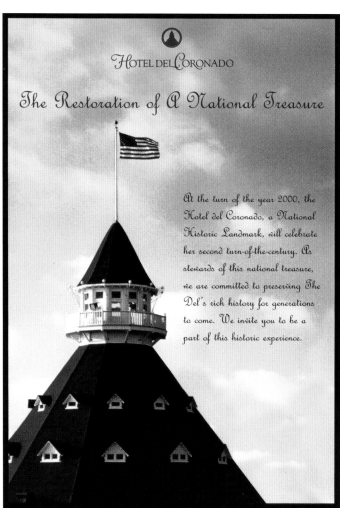

HOTEL DEL CORONADO

The Restoration of A National Treasure

At the turn of the year 2000, the Hotel del Coronado, a National Historic Landmark, will celebrate her second turn-of-the-century. As stewards of this national treasure, we are committed to preserving The Del's rich history for generations to come. We invite you to be a part of this historic experience.

THIS PAGE

At the turn of the 21st century, the Hotel del Coronado unveiled an ambitious and long-range restoration effort (left), which included the installation of Windsor Lawn (above) and the addition of Beach Village (top).

The large expanse of Windsor Lawn — which would have been a typical Victorian resort amenity — replaced tennis court fencing that had obstructed pedestrians' views of the ocean. Beach Village offers luxury accommodations in a private setting, ideal for celebrities or other guests who want an exclusive vacation experience.

THIS PAGE

Today's Del is often tied to the past, as exemplified by the Soden family. Stephanie and Robert Soden (pictured at top) are fifth-generation Del devotees. Their great-great-grandfather, Kansas City resident Peter Soden, started the tradition at least as early as 1903, when the visit he and his wife made was noted in the San Diego society pages.

Son John W. honeymooned at The Del in 1906 (second generation, pictured above with wife, Etta, at the time of their wedding). Their union produced five children (third generation), and by the mid-1930s, the extended Soden clan was part of an established "Kansas City Colony" who summered at The Del year after year. Jack Soden (fourth generation and father of Stephanie and Robert), along with his older brother Stephen (pictured at right with their parents c. 1956), remembers "practically growing up" at the hotel.

Around the Resort

Inviting Interiors

The Lobby

An 1888 Hotel del Coronado brochure — 30 pages in length, with a number of full-page photos — spoke to the comfort of the lobby, which was called the rotunda:

> This is a handsome apartment, large and lofty. Raised high over it, and running all around it, is a wide gallery which commands a view of the floor of the rotunda, where the main office is. This gallery is much frequented by the ladies. Thither they resort for friendly, social converse, and to see newcomers entering below and registering their names.

> The ceiling of the rotunda, which is artistically paneled in oak, has a fine, rich, home-like appearance, and harmonizes well with the beautiful, velvet-like old style of frescoing adopted in the ornamentation of the walls.

Although the lobby has changed over the years, its main configuration has remained the same, including its second-floor balcony. The lobby's elevator was also an original amenity; during a trial run, a reported 2,500 pounds were easily conveyed. Another test proved equally successful: "Two glasses of water were placed on the floor of the cage, and when it dropped, the safety clamps caught it so smoothly that not a drop was spilled."

Original Guestrooms

When the Hotel Del opened in 1888, a San Diego promotional brochure described "an entirely new design or arrangement of rooms and suites," with every room boasting a "court corridor" (courtyard-facing balcony) or "outside veranda" (exterior-facing balcony). "The suites of rooms are grouped around sitting rooms, giving every suite of four or five rooms a special reception sitting room," all with fireplaces and "richly carved mantels with large French bevel-plate mirrors."

> The five hundred guestrooms of the mammoth hotel are all large, well ventilated and lighted, the sun reaching every room in the house at some hour of the day, a feature made possible by architectural design and the diagonal location of the house. The chambers are laid with rug carpets, in Wilton and body Brussels. The furniture comprises mahogany, cherry, oak and sycamore, of the handsomest designs. The windows are shaded with Venetian blinds and draped with coin Swiss curtains.

> Across the top of every dresser is a 72-inch scarf, on which rests a handsome satin antique lace-covered pin cushion. On the center table in each room is also a scarf, upon which rests a silver tray holding a bottle containing frozen water and two cut glass tumblers. Each room also contains a handsome couch.

> The handsomest guestroom in the house is, of course, the bridal chamber. This apartment is furnished in solid natural mahogany, the prevailing colors of upholstery and tapestry being pale blue and cream. The draperies are pale-blue silk, fringed and fastened with old gold and blue.

The "five hundred" guestrooms is not strictly accurate since this total probably included adjoining parlors and possibly even private bathrooms. According to the earliest blueprints, there were about 425 "bedrooms" in the original building.

By contemporary standards, the hotel's approximately 71 bathrooms (bathtubs) and 71 water closets (toilets) hardly seem adequate, but in 1888, private bathrooms were a luxury, and The Del was proud of its inventory. An 1888 hotel brochure drew special attention to its bathing facilities: "On every floor there are several bathrooms with abundance of hot and cold fresh soft water [and] hot and cold saltwater," in which Victorians enjoyed soaking.

By 1900, the hotel was installing an additional 80 "bathrooms," either combining bathing and toilet facilities into one room or adding significantly to its separate bathing rooms.

Additional Accommodations

That same year, Tent City opened, which increased The Del's summer accommodations, although the tents did not offer the same conveniences — such as indoor plumbing — of the "big hotel."

Continued on page 90

PREVIOUS PAGE
The hotel lobby in 1938, the year of The Del's 50th anniversary.

FACING PAGE
An early photo of the lobby-level seating areas. In the early days, the lobby also featured "an immense old English fireplace, 22 feet in width."

The number of guestrooms in the Victorian building has more or less remained constant through the years; however, the addition of bathrooms and the removal of fireplaces, along with some accommodating construction during World War II (when the hotel housed Navy officers) and after (when the hotel allowed its residential guests to make over their own suites of rooms) may have resulted in more or fewer guestrooms. A restoration effort in 2000 combined some smaller rooms, and today the number of guestrooms in the Victorian Building is 368.

The Hotel del Coronado increased its guestroom inventory with Ocean Towers in 1973 and California Cabanas in 1979, adding another 214 and 97 rooms. And in 2007 — long after Elisha Babcock had envisioned adding individual beach cottages to the hotel's property — The Del created Beach Village, with 78 luxury beachside accommodations that can be configured into one-, two- or three-bedroom suites, featuring open living rooms with kitchen/dining areas, oversized baths, fireplaces and intimate outdoor spaces.

Looking Back

Guests frequently ask if there is any original furniture at The Del, but none exists. Hotels are in the business of keeping current, and as soon as the 1888 furnishings began to appear worn or passé, they were no doubt replaced (the son of one former manager remembers his mother making bedside lamps out of 19th-century china pots). Fortunately, enough memorabilia — photos, brochures and personal reminiscences — has been set aside over the years so that the history of the hotel's décor can be documented.

THIS PAGE AND FACING PAGE
In the early days, the lobby level included a variety of alcove rooms for quiet pursuits. As their names indicate, many of these rooms were for ladies, who presumably wouldn't have participated in more robust outdoor activities, including most sports.

Ladies Reception Room And Billiard Parlor Hotel Del Coronado

Reading Room Hotel Del Coronado

Ladies White And Gold Parlor Hotel Del Coronado

Ladies Balcony looking

View From Lobby - Hotel del Coronado.

Lobby, Hotel del Coronado

THIS PAGE AND FACING PAGE
The Del's lobby is always changing. This page, counterclockwise from top: 1920, 1934 and c. 1940. Facing page, counterclockwise from top: c. 1955, c. 1960 and 1993.

AMERICA'S GRAND ALL THE YEAR ROUND SEA SIDE RESORT AND SANITARIUM.

Bridal Chamber.

HOTEL DEL CORONADO, SAN DIEGO COUNTY, CALIFORNIA.

TURNER'S ELITE STUDIO COR. FIFTH AND F STS., SAN DIEGO, CAL.   LARGEST COLLECTION OF VIEWS IN THE CITY.

...do, Bridal Chamber

THIS PAGE

It is likely that the hotel debuted with more than one bridal chamber, and according to a February 13, 1888, article in the San Diego Union, *some artwork was still en route: "Two fine flower pieces in oil, painted to order by Miss M.L. Arlington of Boston, a lady of great repute … are for the bridal chambers and are entitled 'Watching and Waiting' and 'Alone at Last.'"*

THIS PAGE
*By the late 1920s/early 1930s, the hotel's guestrooms
had changed considerably.*

In October 1935, President and Mrs. Franklin Roosevelt occupied the Presidential Suite, which they found "a charming double suite, radiating a warmth and cheerfulness … a homey atmosphere and a pleasing simplicity. The reception hall was perhaps richest in appointment — handsome antique furniture, brocades, oriental rugs and gold-framed mirrors."

Shown here: the entrance to the suite, the sun porch ("decorated to receive the two most eminent citizens of the country") and a private dining room.

FACING PAGE
A well-appointed suite in the 1970s.

THIS PAGE ABOVE
A 1975 guestroom.

THIS PAGE RIGHT
*By contemporary standards, this 1974 Victorian Building
guestroom seems dated and sparsely furnished, but for
Barbara and Larry Guevara, who spent their 26th wedding
anniversary at the hotel, the $32 room ("stretching our
budget") did not disappoint. Remembers Barbara: "We were
shown the prettiest room I had ever seen ... in a cupola with
a garden view. All white wicker with windows on three sides
and a gentle breeze ruffling the curtains. The bathroom floor
was laid with old 1-inch octagonal tiles, and everything was as
cheerful and clean as a spring day in May."*

Dining In

In the late 19th century, a hotel was defined by its "table" or culinary expertise. An 1888 Hotel Del brochure described the resort's culinary department as "one of the most complete, best arranged and most perfectly appointed ever attached to a hotel."

The brochure also described the original dining room (today called the Crown Room): "The grandeur, beauty and chastened elegance of the dining room fill the beholder with an astounding admiration, with neither post nor pillar to interrupt the view." An early San Diego promotional brochure listed the dining room's auxiliary spaces, including a carving room, dish pantries, fruit pantries, bakeshop and pastry room.

The Crown Room's adjoining Coronet Room — then called the Breakfast Room — was praised by the *San Diego Union*: "The room is a marvel of beauty and elegance. The lofty ceilings, large plate-glass windows, rich carpets and the general arrangement make it one of the most attractive in the hotel [with tables] covered with snowy linen, upon which glitters a wealth of cut glass and silverware." There were also four private dining rooms, an open-air café and a separate nurses' and children's dining hall, "fitted and furnished in the same style as the other dining rooms."

The Table

When it came to the table itself, the Hotel del Coronado displayed the best of the best.

> The chinaware is all French, decorated, manufactured in Limoges, France, and all the ware is stamped with the name of the hotel, encircled by a crown. The glassware was made to order in Belgium, and is of the finest cut glass. The linens of the house were made to special order, including several entirely new designs in Scotland.

The hotel's dining service was also praised, with a staff of 80 waiters imported from Boston, New York and Chicago.

Food Sources

In 1888, San Diego couldn't supply the amount of food The Del required; some was imported all the way from San Francisco. Fortunately, Coronado had ample small game and big fish, and the

Continued on page 102

RIGHT
The hotel's main dining room in 1888.

hotel had its own produce garden, as noted in a November 1887 newspaper article: "One of the handsomest spots on the Beach is the garden belonging to the Company, where the vegetables to supply the tables for the hotel will be raised." This was supplemented by Elisha Babcock's nearby ranch, stocked with a variety of fruit trees. A January 1888 guest letter paid tribute to the region's ability to provide fresh produce:

> It's very nice to see all kinds of fruits and vegetables growing at this season. I see oranges ripe and blossoms all on the same tree. I have been walking around today and have seen almost anything you could mention growing — oranges, apples, figs, grapes, pears, olives, bananas, limes, apricots and everything in the vegetable line that grows.

Dining Room Changes

In 1929, the Coronet Room was enlarged by incorporating verandas into the interior, and in later years, the fireplaces were removed from the Crown and Coronet Rooms. By 1940, the Crown Room's original windows had been replaced with larger plate-glass windows, expanding the views.

Throughout the 1950s and into the 1960s, The Del was still on the American plan, and Crown Room employees were expected to serve three meals a day, with time off between each meal. For servers who did not live nearby, the hotel provided dormitory housing, the cost for which was deducted from employee paychecks. For an additional fee, servers could take their meals at the hotel. As one waitress remembered, "In those days, guests 'dined,' and took their time" (accordingly, the wait staff was discouraged even from wearing their *own* watches).

Lengthy vacations were still common, and each party was assigned a specific dining table, having the same waiter throughout their stay. The most prized Crown Room real estate — the window area overlooking the front lawn — was known as the "Gold Coast," and high-rolling patrons "bought" their tables in this section by generously tipping the maître d'. Crown Room guests still dressed for meals, and dinnertime was always black tie.

After the hotel phased out the American plan, the Crown Room became the main restaurant, serving three meals a day. In later years, with guests' preference for seaside dining, the resort's restaurants were established along Windsor Lawn, with the Crown Room reserved for special-occasion dining, including holiday celebrations and Sunday brunch.

Throughout the years, additional restaurants added to the resort's dining options, including:

Silver Grill: Popular in the 1920s and 1930s, the Silver Grill was open during the winter season only and offered weekly dinner dances. A lengthy 1924 *San Diego Union* article attested to the social significance of its season, "a sort of trumpet call for winter's pleasure seekers to begin their merrymaking in earnest."

Luau Room: Opened c. 1955 in the space later occupied by the Prince of Wales Grille, the Luau Room offered Hawaiian ambience with thatched walls, colored lights and a Cantonese/Hawaiian menu.

Prince of Wales Grille: Named for The Del's historic 1920 visitor, the restaurant opened in 1970, drawing a personal letter from the former prince (by then the Duke of Windsor): "The Duchess, who knows the hotel, and I have studied the Grille Room menu voraciously and would like to congratulate the hotel chef on his choice of the succulent fare he offers."

Crown Room Entertainment

In the early years, musical entertainment was a daily occurrence in the Crown Room, where a small orchestra performed on a balcony, usually for lunch and dinner. This tradition — like so many others in the Crown Room — continued well into the 20th century, and World War II guests remember lovely live musical performances during evening meals. During the 1970s, the Crown Room was the site for weekly dinner dances, although for the most part, dancing took place in the Ballroom.

Ballroom Entertainment

Sometimes called the theater, the Ballroom was conceived as the centerpiece of the hotel's social life and outfitted to impress.

> It is circular in shape and commands a view of the beach and the ocean. In it there are frequent entertainments, and the manager gives the guests a hop at least twice a week, the music being supplied by the fine band. In the center of the room, a circular space, 240 feet in circumference, forms the dancing floor, and this space is encompassed by a promenade 20 feet wide. No better arrangement could be desired by those who delight to "trip it on the light fantastic toe."

A c. 1908 hotel brochure included a Ballroom photo with text boasting about The Del's elite social life, which was populated with San Diego's Navy officers, many of whom hailed from America's most prominent families.

> The waters of San Diego have long been the rendezvous for the ships of the United States Navy on duty with the Pacific Squadron. It is also a port of call for the ships of the British and other foreign navies visiting. These features do much to give Coronado its unique reputation as a social center.

In the 1930s, the Ballroom offered dances on Saturday nights, with "top entertainers and dancing until 1 a.m." Ballroom dances continued into the 1960s.

Vintage Entertainment Venues

Casino: Adjoining the Silver Grill Restaurant, the Casino was a favorite New Year's Eve party place, with 400 guests expected in 1921. That evening also featured a nine-piece orchestra and "Supper de Luxe," with a "varied program of entertainment [keeping] guests in the jolliest mood possible." In 1932, the Casino offered dancing from 10:30 p.m. until 2 a.m., with a buffet supper served at 11:30 for $1 per person.

Circus Room: Opened c. 1938, the Circus Room was among San Diego's go-to watering holes during World War II and remained a popular hangout into the 1950s. During the 1940s, Arthur Murray, the internationally known ballroom dancing instructor, was contracted by the Hotel Del. Along with wife Kathryn, he held classes, gave parties and brightened the Circus Room with his fancy footwork.

Ocean View Room: After World War II, the Ocean View Room was added as a dancing venue ("no cover — no minimum").

RIGHT
An 1897 menu (top) and partial wine list (bottom).

ABOVE
Circus Room c. 1955.

Temperature at noon to-day was 65°

✦ DINNER ✦

Oysters on Shell

Mock Turtle   Consomme Volaille, Sevigne

Olives   Radishes   Celery   Caviar
Sweet Pickled Figs

Salmon, Shrimp Sauce
Potato Croquettes   Sliced Tomatoes

Boiled Leg of Mutton with Turnips

Filet of Beef, Pique, with Stuffed Tomato
Small Patties of Chicken a l'Imperiatrice
Sweetbreads Braisee with Green Peas
Fresh Mushrooms on Toast

Sorbet de Prince

Ribs of Beef   Roast Ham, Champagne Sauce
Roast Turkey

Mashed Potatoes   Boiled Potatoes
Cauliflower   Spinach   Asparagus   Boiled Rice
Stewed Tomatoes

Shrimp Salad   Celery Mayonnaise

English Plum Pudding, Hard and Brandy Sauce
Mince Pie

Biscuit a la Reine   Champagne Jelly

Coronado Pudding Glace
Assorted Cakes
Confectionery

Fruit   Nuts   Pine Nuts   Raisins   Snowflakes
Roquefort, Swiss and American Cheese
Coffee

Guests are requested to be in the dining room at an early hour.
No seats reserved after 6:30 o'clock

MEAL HOURS — Breakfast, 6 to 10.30.   Lunch, 12 to 2   Dinner, 6.00 to 8.00
Nurses and Children   "   6 to 9   12 to 1.30   "   5.30 to 7

SUNDAY, FEBRUARY 28, 1897.

PROGRAM.
TREV. SHARP, Musical Director

March—Oriental Echoes	. . Rosey
Overture—The Emperor	Kiesler
Song—The Holy City (Adams)	. arr. Sharp
Selection—Maritana	Wallace
Canzonette—Felice	Langey
Valse Caprice—A Sweet Dream .	Eilenberg
Hallelujah Chorus—Messiah	. Handel

⤜HOTEL DEL CORONADO WINES⤛
Coronado Natural Mineral Water, qts. 25c., pts. 15c.
WE INVITE COMPARISON WITH APOLLINARIS.

CHAMPAGNES

	pts.	qts.		pts.	qts.
Roederer, white |& br'n l'bl	$2 50	$4 50	Perrier Jouet, ½-pts, $1 25		
G. H. Mumm, Extra Dry	2 50	4 50	Veuve Clicquot (yellow l'bl)	2 50	4 50
Pommery Sec.	2 50	4 50	Moet Chandon White * Seal	2 50	4 50
Perrier, Jouet, ex.dry	2 50	4 50	Eclipse, extra dry (Calif.) .	1 00	2 00

PURE CALIFORNIA WINES.
Specially selected and bottled for Hotel del Coronado.

SONOMA VINEYARDS.

Zinfandel, Coronado	25	50	Choice California Sauterne	50	1 00
Zinfandel, 1884	50	1 00	Reisling . .	25	50
Burgundy	50	1 00	Reisling (old) .	50	1 00
Burgundy—Chablis (white)	50	1 00	Madeira .	50	1 00

J. GUNDLACH & CO.

Burgundy—Chablis (white)	50	1 00	Cabinet Gutedel	50	1 00
Sauterne	50	1 00	Cabinet Framiner	50	1 00
Chateau Yquem .	75	1 50	Reisling	50	1 00
Semillon . .	50	1 00			

SUNNY SLOPE VINEYARDS (L. J ROSE.)

Port Wine	50	1 00	Angelica	50	1 00
Sherry	50	1 00	Sherry, extra choice	75	1 50

SCHRAMSBERG VINEYARD.

Hock	50	1 00	Zinfandel . .	50	1 00
Burgundy	50	1 00	Reisling	50	1 00

CHAS. A. WETMORE CO., LIVERMORE, CAL., CRESTA BLANCA SOUVENIR VINTAGES

SAUTERNES.			CLARET		
Sauterne, Souvenir .	50	1 00	Table d'Hote, Souvenir	50	1 00
Haut Sauterne, 1887, Souv'r	1 00	2 00	St. Julien	75	1 50
Chateau Yquem, 1886 "	1 25	2 50	Margeaux "	1 00	2 00

TABLE WINE—"Carignan" $ .50 $1.00

THIS PAGE
*A photograph of a ladies' luncheon (top) included in a
c. 1925 hotel brochure carried the caption "Open-Air
Luncheon on the Ocean Terrace in Winter." The brochure
also featured the children's dining room (left) and the
interior of the Garden Patio's "Summer House" (above).*

THE MANAGEMENT OF HOTEL DEL CORONADO
ANNOUNCES THE ENGAGEMENT OF
VIC MYERS AND HIS FAMOUS ORCHESTRA
FOR THE SEASON OF 1923-1924
COMMENCING DECEMBER TWENTY-SECOND

THIS ORCHESTRA WAS ONE OF THREE ON THE PACIFIC COAST CHOSEN BY THE BRUNSWICK-
BALKE-COLLENDER COMPANY TO MAKE THEIR DANCE RECORDS---"NUF SED"
Ask to hear their first record, "Mean, Mean Mama" and "Shake It and Break It", at any Brunswick Phonograph Agency.

Your presence is requested

at the

Hotel del Coronado
Follies of 1926

On the Evening of Wednesday, March Seventeenth
Nineteen Hundred Twenty-six
At Nine o'Clock
For the Benefit of the Boys' Dormitory at Rest Haven
Admission Two Dollars

THE MANAGEMENT OF HOTEL DEL CORONADO
REQUESTS THE HONOR OF YOUR
PRESENCE AT A
BLACK AND WHITE BALL
TO BE GIVEN IN THE BALLROOM
SATURDAY, JANUARY THE TWENTY-SEVENTH
AT NINE O'CLOCK

COSTUMES BLACK, WHITE, OR BLACK AND WHITE
ONLY THOSE IN COSTUME ALLOWED ON THE
FLOOR UNTIL TEN-THIRTY

THIS PAGE
*A variety of dining and entertainment invitations and
announcements from the 1920s.*

. . . the Ocean Terrace Room

Coronado's latest innovation . . . Smart with splashing color . . . the blue Pacific stretching westward almost at your very feet » » » » Such is the new Ocean Terrace Room where traditions of half a century carry on in a modern setting.

Hotel del Coronado
Coronado, California

Hotel del Coronado
Coronado Beach
California

Announces Opening
of the

Silver Grill

For Winter Season,
Monday Evening, December 24th
with a

Dinner Dance de Luxe
Commencing at 7 o'clock
Jimmie Kerr's Casino Orchestra Playing
$3.00 per Person, Including Couvert

Please Make Table Reservations Early
MEL S. WRIGHT, Manager

THIS PAGE ABOVE
Adjoining the hotel's historic bar, the Ocean Terrace Room was opened in the late 1930s, serving up drinks and dancing. Its popularity continued well into the 1950s, and during the 1954 Christmas season, guests were invited to dance to the orchestra of Howard Everett. Afterward, a candlelight supper was offered in the Coronet Room. Originally a lounge, the Ocean Terrace eventually included its own dining facilities.

THIS PAGE RIGHT
A Silver Grill announcement, c. 1930.

FACING PAGE
Despite the constraints of the Depression, the Hotel del Coronado produced some beautifully rendered dining pieces in the 1930s, including a lovely doily (bottom left).

HOTEL del CORONADO
CORONADO BEACH CALIFORNIA

LUNCHEON

Sunkist Cocktail

Soup
Rice Tomato
Jellied Chicken Gumbo   Consomme, in Cups

Relishes
Sliced Cucumbers
Green Onions   Mustard Pickles

Fish
Sand Dabs Saute, Meuniere
Potatoes Julienne

Entrees
Sugar Cured Corned Beef and Cabbage
Potted Turkey Wings and Smothered Celery
Welsh Rarebit
Lemon Sherbet

From the Broiler—Cooked to Order
Saddle of Lamb (wait 5 minutes)
Deviled Legs of Spring Chicken with Bacon

Potatoes
Steamed   Macaire

Vegetables
Creamed Spinach
Fresh String Beans
Buttered White Onions
Baked Zuchini, Provencale   Wheatena

Cold Meats
Roast Beef   Ham   Tongue   Lamb   Salami
Corned Beef   Head Cheese   French Sardines
Goose Liver Pate   Pickled Pig's Feet

Salad
Hotel del Coronado Special Bowl
Hearts of Lettuce
Cottage Cheese

Sweets
Blueberry Pie   Devil Food Cake
Apple Tapioca Pudding, Cream Sauce
Gage Plums in Syrup
Cinnamon Coffee Buns

Fresh Fruits
Oranges   Apples   Bananas   Cherries
Apricots   Watermelon
Assorted Cheese   Crackers
Tea   Coffee   Milk   Refreshing Iced Tea
Fresh Churned Buttermilk

Monday, June 10, 1935

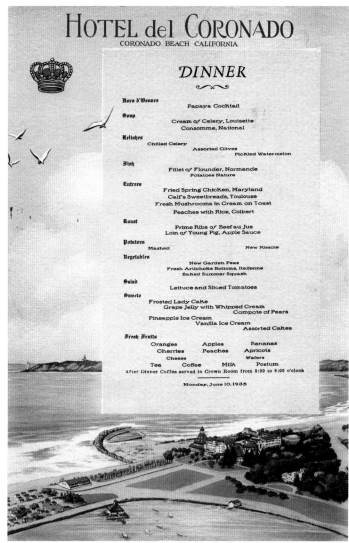

HOTEL del CORONADO
CORONADO BEACH CALIFORNIA

DINNER

Hors d'Oeuvre   Papaya Cocktail

Soup
Cream of Celery, Louisette
Consomme, National

Relishes
Chilled Celery
Assorted Olives
Pickled Watermelon

Fish
Fillet of Flounder, Normande
Potatoes Nature

Entrees
Fried Spring Chicken, Maryland
Calf's Sweetbreads, Toulouse
Fresh Mushrooms in Cream on Toast
Peaches with Rice, Colbert

Roast
Prime Ribs of Beef au Jus
Loin of Young Pig, Apple Sauce

Potatoes
Mashed   New Rissole

Vegetables
New Garden Peas
Fresh Artichoke Bottoms, Italienne
Baked Summer Squash

Salad
Lettuce and Sliced Tomatoes

Sweets
Frosted Lady Cake
Grape Jelly with Whipped Cream
Compote of Pears
Pineapple Ice Cream
Vanilla Ice Cream
Assorted Cakes

Fresh Fruits
Oranges   Apples   Bananas
Cherries   Peaches   Apricots
Cheese   Wafers
Tea   Coffee   Milk   Postum
After Dinner Coffee served in Crown Room from 8:00 to 9:00 o'clock

Monday, June 10, 1935

ANNOUNCING
Buffet Supper
at no extra charge
at the
Saturday Night
Casino Dances

$1

All inclusive

Dancing
10:30 till 2
Buffet Supper
11 to 1
Late Ferries
1:50 A.M.

Hotel del
CORONADO

Musical Program

"On the Beautiful Blue Danube"	*Johann Strauss*
Gems from Stephen Foster—	
Old Black Joe	
Beautiful Dreamer	
Oh! Susanna	
Jeanie with the Light Brown Hair	
De Camptown Races	
Melody in F	*Anton Rubenstein*
Selections from "Naughty Marietta"	*Victor Herbert*
Emperor Waltz	*Johann Strauss*
Memories of the Gay Nineties—	
School Days	
You Had a Dream, Dear	
Wait Till the Sun Shines Nellie	
In the Good Old Summer Time	
By the Light of the Silvery Moon	
After the Ball	
I Want a Girl	
The Sidewalks of New York	
Selections from "The Merry Widow"	*Franz Lehar*
Serenade	*Franz Schubert*
Voices of Spring	*Johann Strauss*
Selections from "The Prince of Pilsen"	*Gustav Luders*

Anniversary Dinner 60

Supreme of Fruit au Maraschino   Chilled Sweet Cider

Clear Green Turtle Amontillado   Cream of Tomatoes Brestoise

Melba Toast

Hearts of Utah Celery   Choice California Olives

Salted Almonds   Iced Carrotsticks   Spiced Melonrind

Casserolettes of Point Loma Lobster
in Cream and Brandy a la Maryland

Unjointed Milkfed Chicken saute aux Champignons
Roast Saddle of Nevada Lamb, sauce Poivrade
Oregon Tom Turkey with Oyster Dressing   Cranberry Jelly
Filet Mignon Grille a la Bearnaise

Potatoes Rissoles   Candied Southern Yams
Steamed Wild Rice in Butter
Green Asparagus Polonaise   Mint Flavored New Peas
Silver Skin Onions in Cream

Cracked Wheat Bread   Dinner Rolls   Rye Bread

Hearts of Iceberg Lettuce   Sliced Avocado
Peach and Cottage Cheese Hawaiienne
French Dressing   Roquefort Dressing   Maraschino Dressing

Mocca Parfait   Black Walnut Layer Cake   Coupe St. Jacques
Cocoanut Cream Pie   Coronado Petits-Fours   Almond Macaroons
Stewed Fresh Pineapple

Winter Pears   Delicious Apples   Tangerines
Bananas   Grapes   Dried Figs   Cluster Raisins

Wisconsin Blue Cheese   Camembert   Old English Cheese

Cafe Noir

Chocolate Mint Wafers

Thursday, February 19, 1948

July Fourth
1 9 4 4

Hotel del Coronado
CORONADO, CALIFORNIA

The 1944 Fourth of July menu included the preamble to the Constitution, along with an announcement for "Meatless Day for Victory." There was also a reference to the Office of Price Administration (established by President Franklin Roosevelt to stabilize prices during World War II): "All prices listed are at or below our ceiling prices … by OPA regulations."

In 1948, the hotel celebrated its 60th birthday with a special anniversary menu and musical program.

THIS PAGE
Clockwise from bottom left: The Terrace Room; a banjo player in the Circus Room; and The Del's bar, all c. 1940/1945.

RIGHT
A c. 1940 multi-page Del cocktail menu included this poignant quote: "Time flies, you say? Oh, no — Time stays; we go" (a variation of lines from a poem by Englishman Henry Austin Dobson).

Mixed Drinks

Tom Collins	.40
John Collins	.40
Whiskey Sour	.40
Rum Sour	.50
Rum Collins	.50
Cuban Libre	.50
Tequila Sour	.50
Brandy Sour	.50, .75
Brandy Flip	.65, .85
Horse's Neck	.50
Sherry Flip	.50
Gin and Tonic	.60
Singapore Sling	.60
Egg Nogg	.65
Horse's Neck (with Brandy)	.75
Planter's Punch	.75
Tequila Sunrise	.75
Mint Julep	1.00
Mint Julep (Southern Comfort)	1.00
Zombie	1.50
French "75"	2.00

Fizzes

Gin Fizz	.40
Sloe Gin Fizz	.40
Gin Rickey	.40
Sloe Gin Rickey	.40
Golden Fizz	.50
Royal Fizz	.50
Silver Fizz	.50
New Orleans Fizz	.75
Brandy Fizz	.75

The Casino Lounge

THIS PAGE
Scenes from the 1950s and 1960s include the colorful Circus
Room (top left), a dancing demonstration (bottom left), the
Casino Lounge (top right) and an artist's conception of the
proposed Ballroom renovation (bottom right).

TOP

The Luau Room was a popular restaurant for many years (above right), and the c. 1965 menu (above left) featured exotic drinks such as Tahitian club punch, pelisco, Pango Pango cocktail and Bimini cooler, along with the recipes for each. The shark's tooth cocktail was composed of 1½ ounces of Tanduay rum, 1 ounce of lemon juice and passion fruit, and ½ ounce of sloe gin.

RIGHT

During the Crown Room's mid-century heyday, guests still dressed for dinner.

Daily Delights

The Hotel del Coronado debuted as a destination resort, offering every necessity and luxury its upper-class clientele demanded (in 1888, San Diego was a small city, unable to aid in the hotel's hospitality efforts). The turn-of-the-century guests stayed for months at a time, so the resort could not afford to run short on anything. Accordingly, The Del offered pragmatic amenities, such as a well-stocked newsstand, as well as a varied inventory of guest diversions. As a c. 1900 brochure pointed out, "A special effort is made to see that every moment of one's stay has been well and happily spent."

On-Site Amenities

In the early days, the hotel hosted a variety of interesting guest attractions, including a labyrinth; museum (with "10,000 interesting specimens ... the finest collection west of Philadelphia"); curio bazaar (offering "interesting exhibits of curiosities from Arizona, New and Old Mexico and the Pacific Coast"); botanical gardens (about 10 blocks away); Japanese tea garden ("considered the most celebrated piece of work of its kind on this continent"); and darkrooms for amateur photographers.

The hotel's electrical works and ice plant were also a draw, "seen to fine advantage in the evening," and in-house tours were offered for guests "who desire to be shown through the building, including the kitchen, bakery and cold storages." A nearby ostrich farm (a typical Victorian attraction) rounded out the more-immediate offerings; the hotel also boasted its own display of monkeys and deer. And for guests interested in indoor entertainment, rooms were available for cards, chess, music, reading, writing and smoking.

Children at The Del

When it came to children, the Victorian period was an era of "seen but not heard." Especially in America's wealthiest families, children were relegated to separate areas of houses and spent most of their time with nannies; often, offspring weren't integrated into a family's everyday adult life until they were older and ready for "society," usually at marriageable ages. At The Del, this preferred separation of generations was reflected in guestroom arrangements (suites of rooms so children could sleep with their nannies) and in dining facilities (a separate dining room for children and their caretakers).

Parents, meanwhile, enjoyed a relatively adults-only vacation, which included leisurely meals in the Crown Room, an array of recreational activities and endless social soirées — none of them geared toward children. But even under these conditions, the turn-of-the-century Del was a child's paradise: Vacations were lengthy, and children no doubt settled into a relaxed routine, where one delightful day drifted into another.

An early children-only amenity may have been instituted in 1893, when a newspaper referenced a new "recreation room" off the Garden Patio, complete with "all sorts of games for the little ones, and with couches for naps, and soft carpets to break the frail folks' frequent falls."

The hotel's Beach School, added in the early 1900s, took some of the pressure off home schooling for nannies and parents. A guest account from 1918 attested to its success: "In the morning, all groups of children are around having lessons in French. A dozen little tots have kindergarten." Serving Coronado residents as well as hotel guests, the Beach School provided K–12 instruction in open-air tents and cottages. Reportedly, a young Howard Hughes was in attendance c. 1920, as were the offspring of Enrico Caruso.

Turn-of-the-Century Sightseeing

An 1891 hotel brochure titled "Memoranda of Pleasant Places which Guests May Easily Visit" touted the region's sights, including The Del's own rail line "around the bay"; the Coronado Islands, "enjoyed either in a yacht or by a small steamer"; the Sweetwater Dam; Old Town, the original San Diego city site; La Jolla, "noted for its weird caves" ("by carriage"); Point Loma "with its fine lighthouse"; the El Cajon Valley "with its wonderful production" of produce; desert destinations, a novelty for most Americans; and Tijuana, "our sister Republic of Mexico."

Nearby Naval Air Station North Island was accessible for Del guests, who were invited to attend weekly receptions "on board the cruisers of the Pacific." That early guests were considered more in residence than on vacation was reflected in the hotel's mention of the Lakeside Inn, "an excellent hotel," offered as a side trip during a Del stay.

Continued on page 114

FACING PAGE
*A c. 1925 hotel activities brochure highlighted everything
from formal dances to moving pictures, concerts,
bridge games and afternoon tea.*

HOTEL del CORONADO
Coronado Beach, Cal.

Its Social
Activities
and
Entertainment
Features

A Day at The Del in 1919

A guest program for Wednesday, August 6, 1919, speaks to the incredible choice of activities offered (both social and recreational), mentioning an afternoon tea in the Rose Palm Room; a midweek dance in the Casino; the availability of the "Chaplin Air Line Curtiss Flying Boat ... for those desiring to view the Pacific from the air"; riding on "fine saddle horses"; a library near the elevator; motor touring "made safe and comfortable in cars of the Hotel Auto Service"; after-dinner coffee on the veranda; private instruction in "modern ballroom dancing"; shopping in the hotel's Japanese art shop or in its satellite I. Magnin store; and for the amateur photographer, Harold A. Taylor's Art Room offered "Kodak films developed and printed."

A guest letter sent a year earlier referenced a myriad of sightseeing, including the San Diego exposition grounds, aviation field (North Island), Ramona's marriage place and Point Loma. The letter also mentioned Marine band performances twice a day and three dances a week. Another guest from the same time period (according to his descendants), had his Pierce-Arrow transported by ship from Washington State using it to tour San Diego sights and becoming very popular with other guests, few of whom vacationed with their automobiles.

Into the '30s

A 1931 remodeling of the Ballroom accommodated contemporary entertainments, including "moving pictures, vaudeville performances, costume balls and all the various entertainments, which are a part of the regular winter program." The Del also promoted bridge parties in the '30s, although the game of whist — a precursor to bridge — was mentioned as early as the turn of the century, its many Del fans referred to as "fiends." A guest program for the week of June 21, 1931, referenced keno (a bingo-type game), complimentary rides aboard the "gasoline" launch *Glorietta*, swimming instruction, the Japanese tea garden, tennis, and dancing lessons. Hotel amenities included thrice-daily mail delivery, a hotel physician, hairdressing parlors, a Western Union telegraph office, "electric cabinet Turkish baths," offices for Logan & Bryan (members of the New York Stock Exchange), "complete valet service" for gentlemen, and a circulating library.

At about the same time, the hotel instituted a "Breakfast Club" for teens and tweens, "whose purpose is good fellowship and to 'keep on smiling.'" According to a *California Life* article, the club — with separate girls' and boys' divisions — met Tuesday mornings, with a swim in the "new" pool, followed by a poolside "repast." Additional activities for club members included horse shows, tours of Navy ships (boys only), horseback rides on the beach, costume parties (a first prize was awarded to "Queen of Coronado," a young girl dressed in a long gown "decorated with crowns and other insignia of the hotel"), and games of musical chairs and pin the tail on the donkey.

Mid-Century Pleasures

Many of these activities continued over the next few decades. A 1963 promotional mailing detailed an array of family entertainment and recreation, including bingo, Ping Pong, volleyball, shuffleboard, beach games, boating (sail, paddle, motor and row), water-skiing, sport fishing, tennis exhibitions and movie nights in the Ballroom. Children had their own Game Room, along with Wednesday morning cartoons and the Children's Summer Sport Club, which provided supervised play and handicrafts as well as instruction in sailing, swimming and diving. There were also kids' classes in croquet, pencil sketching, clay modeling, storybook reading and shell crafts. Teens were offered dances, bicycle tours and scavenger hunts. Adults could choose from hotel tours, barbecues on the beach or moonlight cruises.

State-of-the-Art Spas

By the 1960s, health spas had emerged as a way to attain physical and mental well-being, and The Del debuted its own Del Coronado Spa, offering "unmatched facilities for hydrotherapy, physical condition and relaxation for discriminating men and women ... a new concept for living longer and looking younger." Interestingly, exercise equipment and activities were not mentioned in the spa's offerings; instead, water therapies were highlighted, including a "swirl pool" for hydro massage, a heated immersion pool, pressure showers and a rock steam room.

Massages were also available, as were "cooling lounges," a place for "rest or slumber" (presumably to offset the effort expended undergoing water or massage therapy). Women were offered "complete facilities for facials" at the "beauty bar"; men could partake of a "private clubroom ... a quiet retreat for mental relaxation ... meetings, cards or reading." Soon after, a women's clubroom was also added.

In the next decade or so, The Del's "Health Spa" included a "gymnasium," which would become an "exercise room" by c. 1987, and the spa continued to evolve as fitness fashions dictated. Today, Spa at The Del is an award-winning facility, named one of the top 20 hotel spas in the world by *Travel + Leisure* magazine.

ABOVE
Pictures in a c. 1912 brochure highlighted many of the hotel's guest activities.

The Del as Destination

For San Diego visitors, the Hotel del Coronado was high on the list of sights to see. An 1897 day tourist recounted his experiences in his diary:

> We three hayseeds actually took lunch in the magnificent dining room. We spent the remainder of the day till after seven o'clock in "taking in" the many wonders of Hotel del Coronado. Went out on long iron pier, which projects far out into the ocean, and watched for a while the gigantic billows come rolling in. Visited the hotel's menagerie and beautiful bathhouse. Returning to hotel proper, listened to excellent instrumental concert in spacious concert hall.
>
> After concert we, with characteristic Yankee audacity, tramped all over the great Coronado, from basement to the big cupola from which last point a most magnificent view of ocean and San Diego was obtained. A feature of the Coronado is the great number of parlors and sitting rooms; it has almost as many as the average hotel has rooms of all kinds, and they are all finely furnished too.
>
> Inside inspection over, we promenaded aristocratically round the entire affair, as if we were of that class of people who can afford to pay five dollars a night for a bed. Then ensconced ourselves in elegant rocking chairs on the rotunda surrounding the office and main entrance, and there, in gawking enjoyment, feasting our countrified eyes on the "stylers" as they, in décolleté costumes, majestically tripped down the grand stairway for dinner.
>
> Feeling somewhat out of place in the scene of congregated wealth, we silently stole out into the darkness about 7:30, took the electric car to ferry, and the ferry freighted us back to the mainland of the State of California. San Diego doesn't lavish much illumination on its waterfront, and from the wharf to the center of town, we had to grope our way through [dark] streets.
>
> In contrast to our high-toned lunch, we filled up for supper on 5 cents per bowl restaurant soup, and instead of the five dollar sleeping apartments, we retired, after our fatiguing day's sightseeing, to beds that "set us back" just 33 1/3 cents a piece at the St. James Hotel.

Japanese Tea Garden, Coronado, San Diego, Cal.

Beginning Wednesday evening, December 24,

Talking Pictures

will be shown in the Ballroom of Hotel del Coronado every Monday, Wednesday and Friday evening, during the winter season, starting at eight-fifteen.

Admission fifty cents a person.   Complimentary to dinner guests on those evenings.

The latest Western Electric Sound Equipment has been installed.

THIS PAGE
A c. 1930 "Talking Pictures" announcement (left) and the hotel's Japanese Tea Garden, c. 1915 (above).

FACING PAGE
A sampling of guest activities featured in a 1937 brochure (top right); an activities brochure from 1931 (bottom right); a 1928 ad for the hotel's I. Magnin & Co. store (bottom middle); and a c. 1910 bridge announcement (bottom left).

GOLF

PITCH and PUT Course in the West Gardens. Golf clubs obtainable at the desk.

CORONADO COUNTRY CLUB—Playing privileges are available to guests of the hotel. See Bill Foley, instructor at the Club.

BICYCLING

To obtain bicycles, inquire at the desk.

HORSEBACK RIDING

CORONADO RIDING STABLES—Horses especially suitable for children are available. Inquire at the desk or telephone Coronado 1265-J.

BADMINTON and PING PONG

Racquets may be procured at the desk.

TRAP & SKEET SHOOTING

PASTIME GUN CLUB on Causeway, north of Rosecrans and Barnett Streets in San Diego. Wednesday and Saturday afternoons from 2 to 5 P. M. Sundays from 9 A. M. to 5 P. M. Special parties by appointment. Charge, $1.15 per round including shells and targets. Guns can also be furnished. For further information call Mrs. Heath at Hotel San Diego. Franklin 1221.

[Page 6]

CONTRACT BRIDGE

Supervised bridge and instruction by Mrs. Ahlborn.

THE BEACH SCHOOL

Mrs. Owers is available for tutoring in all subjects. Coronado 237-J.

DANCING

Helen Peddicord, instructor in all phases of dancing.

BEAUTY PARLORS

Located on the Casino Floor on the Ocean Front.

ELECTRIC CABINET BATHS

Steam, Salt Water Baths and massage for men and women. Casino Floor on the Ocean Front.

BARBER SHOP

In the Corridor, Casino Floor.

ROBERT E. AUSTIN, M.D.

Office in the Hotel, Hours 11-12 A. M., 2-4 P. M.

HAROLD A. TAYLOR—

Photographer

Photographs. Kodak films developed and printed.

I. MAGNIN COMPANY

Women's wearing apparel. Lobby floor.

WESTERN UNION

Visit the new office at the south end of the front porch.

[Page 7]

THIS · WEEK

AT

Hotel del Coronado

Coronado Beach, California

MEL S. WRIGHT, Manager

JUNE 21 TO JUNE 27, 1931

THIS PAGE AND FACING PAGE
*In the 1950s and 1960s, fashion shows and beauty
pageants were the rage.*

George Griffiths: The Del's Pacific Pied Piper

With the social changes wrought by World War I and the Roaring Twenties, a new subset of children emerged: the teenager. At The Del, this shift was reflected in the hiring of George Griffiths, a teenager himself, who was tapped to teach swimming and diving to children at Tent City.

Griffiths, who later qualified for the 1932 Olympic tryouts and counted swimmer/actor Johnny Weissmuller as one of his friends, swam at The Del with Esther Williams. He ultimately took over additional children's resort activities and excelled in acrobatic diving, sailing and aquaplaning. His popularity was legendary, and he supervised The Del's athletic and children's programs for decades. Avid admirers remember Griffiths' inspired swimming and diving instruction in the 1950s, at the height of his reign, along with The Del's formalized programs, including a "Summer Sports Club," a mix of boating, handicrafts and other activities. As Melody Locke Evans recalled:

> If the tide allowed, George would steer us right underneath the boathouse into a labyrinth of creosoted pilings crawling with big crabs. We cruised Glorietta Bay, looking at small fish just beneath the surface. The best part was when George landed on the "deserted island," a sandy bank by the golf course. We had swordfights with sticks and imagined ourselves to be pirates or Robinson Crusoe. We loved being shipwrecked! After lunch, the counselors supervised us as we dug on the gold-flecked shore for sand crabs, climbed around the old cement jetties or built castles.

Evans also remembers riding ocean waves, scavenger hunts, sand castle contests, model plane competitions, movies, talent shows and more. A particular favorite was the "penny dive":

> This was no ordinary penny dive, for George had a whole bucketful of money, a veritable fortune, not limited to pennies! We would shriek with delight as we caught the glimmer of silver coins in the sun and carefully followed their wavy descent to the bottom. There was much splashing and thrashing and kicking of feet as we fought to be the first to reach the silver dollars. Finally, when not a speck remained on the blue-tiled bottom, we counted. It was not unusual for me to find nearly twenty dollars' worth of coins; I felt like a millionaire!

Evans' brother, George A. Locke, was likewise transformed by his days with Griffiths. In 1954, concerned about his inability to swim, Locke was buoyed by The Del's saltwater pool, along with his discovery that he "was not to be tossed into the deep end right away and expected to remain afloat." He remembers Griffiths' "well-thought-out plan of attack" and "no-nonsense, businesslike precision" at the shallow end, which resulted in "a credible breaststroke at the deep end" and the ability to execute "simple dives."

Like his sister, George remembered that the Summer Sports Club offered "neither time nor opportunity for boredom." He recalled particularly the "ghost walks" Griffiths offered in the hotel's "labyrinthine basement":

> ... all through the basement complex, encountering piles of stored hotel room furniture and other obstacles, until the central basement corridor finally terminated at a door that led directly into the hotel's kitchen. Images of ghosts and goblins one moment; amused cadres of cooks busily chopping carrots the next.

Locke remembers his summers at The Del under Griffiths' tutelage as an era lost to time:

> Surely the safety zealots of our current age would faint in shock if anybody suggested taking a boatload of young kids under the pilings of the hotel boathouse, or allowing them to trip their way through a darkened hotel basement. The postwar years in which I grew up had some distinct advantages [but] none of what I was able to enjoy during those summer months would have materialized without the energy, enthusiasm, dedication and sheer imagination of George Griffiths.

ABOVE LEFT
This c. 1956 photo of The Del's "Summer Sports Club" includes director George Griffiths helping aboard a young Melody Locke Evans.

ABOVE
George Griffiths, The Del's in-house aquatics instructor, taught many hotel guests and Coronado residents how to execute impressive dives.

THIS PAGE
Fun in the sun with George Griffiths' "Summer Sports Club."

Health Above All

So intertwined were holidays and health for Victorian travelers that The Del promoted itself as a resort and a "sanitarium," where physical well-being could be strengthened or even reclaimed. An 1888 brochure described the hotel as "that spot on Earth where doctors have little employment ... for we breathe the true elixir of life." This was not an exaggeration; compared to the congested urban areas back East, Southern California was remarkably disease-free, and visitors often did fare better in mild, Mediterranean climates, where they could enjoy being out in the fresh air year round.

Exceptional Offerings

The Del offered a variety of outdoor sports that were especially appealing to Victorian tourists:

The Beach: A c. 1890 brochure captured the healthy charm of The Del's beachside setting: "It is the Paradise of the Pacific, the Mecca of tourists in search of rest, health, sport and diversion. 'Tis a land of sunny days, where care is a stranger; where pessimists are born again; where sick people get well." For Victorians, ocean air was considered inherently healthy (especially in the age of tuberculosis), and saltwater was thought to be cleansing for body and mind. An early brochure boasted, "The surf bathing of Coronado Beach is the best on the entire coast and probably the finest in the world ... enjoyed every day in the year; the beach is sandy and gently sloping." Additional Victorian beach pastimes included gathering shells and seaweed, some of which were fashioned into handicrafts.

Boating: Surrounded by ocean and bay, The Del offered a variety of maritime options, along with its own boathouse, equipped with rowboats and sailboats as well as steam yachts. Glass-bottom boats provided an up-close look at Coronado's marine life. And by the 1930s, aquaplaning had become a popular adjunct to boating.

Swimming: Although few Victorians knew how to swim, "taking the waters" was paramount for vacationers who believed that saltwater was restorative and even curative. Accordingly, even before the hotel opened, it offered a bathhouse attached to the original boathouse; more appealing to many than the open sea, it was screened to keep out sea critters. This temporary facility was soon replaced by a permanent structure — a high-ceilinged, windowed building, with 70 changing rooms and separate hot and cold swimming tanks, for which a San Diego newspaper reported variations in temperatures on a daily basis. By 1920, more "gymnastic" features were added, including a slide and rings. Tent City also provided a bayside plunge, as well as a shallow children's pool, at a whopping 100 by 175 feet:

"the finest place for the person unable to swim or who is just learning to do so."

Fishing: An 1891 brochure boasted of "deep-sea fishing from the shore, at all seasons. Fish are very abundant." A 700-foot fishing pier constructed in 1890 made it possible for timid ocean-goers to partake in this exciting sport. Common catches included barracuda, sea bass, yellowtail, mackerel, sea trout, halibut, albacore, flounder, grouper and more. In 1899, the hotel boasted a day's catch of almost 2,000 fish.

Hunting: With Coronado's incredible bounty of small game, The Del was originally promoted as a hunting resort, with "an abundance" of quail, curlew, plovers, ducks, geese, rabbits, and its own supply of hunting hounds. Trap shooting was also available.

Horses: Horses were used for transportation as well as sport (racing along the beach or hunting with the hounds); however, an early racetrack was not a success. According to Elisha Babcock, "It did not pay us to have any attractions of that kind. There generally was swindling going on, and it injured more than it helped us." Later, the Coronado Country Club offered both horseracing and horse shows. Donkey rides — especially on the beach — were also available.

Continued on page 124

Carriage Rides: Touring Coronado or points beyond via horse-driven carriages was a popular turn-of-the-century pursuit, and in 1891, The Del rented carriages and buggies at $3 to $6 per day. A tallyho coach offered a spin in a horse-drawn carriage built for speed, another Victorian "sport."

Polo: In 1906, owner John D. Spreckels added polo to the hotel's offerings via the Coronado Country Club. Populated with international teams, along with a local team comprising mostly Navy officers, polo drew a moneyed crowd to Coronado before World War I depleted its ranks.

Tennis: The hotel's first tennis court, located across Orange Avenue, was in place as early as March 13, 1888, when a *San Diego Union* article referenced its temporary ruination by a horse-drawn carriage. The Del's facilities were soon augmented with courts at the Coronado Country Club. There was also badminton.

Golf: The Coronado Country Club offered golf on its bayview/oceanview course, supplemented by The Del's own putting green and miniature golf course. The Country Club course was 5,318 yards long; "the bunkers and hazards are skill testers."

Coronado Country Club

Established with the support of hotel owner John D. Spreckels, the Coronado Country Club (an independent enterprise, c. 1900) was open to all hotel and Tent City guests, who could pay a daily fee or opt for membership. A center of San Diego's sporting life, the Country Club offered a golf course, polo grounds and tennis courts.

Beach & Tennis Club

In 1934, the hotel's in-ground pool was built, replacing the 19th-century bathhouse. A saltwater sensation, the pool — originally called the Turquoise Pool — was built to Olympic standards and featured a high-diving board. Filled with warmed and filtered ocean water (replaced daily), the pool was surrounded by a sandy area heated by steam pipes beneath the surface. Canvas cabanas were constructed on the far side of the pool, where renters could catch cool ocean breezes.

In response to the growing popularity of tennis, oceanfront courts were added in the 1930s. The hotel's "Beach & Tennis Club" became a popular social outlet for visitors and Coronado residents alike and attracted a slew of professional tennis players, including Maureen Connolly, Pancho Gonzalez, Bobby Riggs, Billie Jean King, Chris Everett and André Agassi.

Into the 1950s and Beyond

Another sport gaining popularity at mid-century was golf, which the city of Coronado accommodated with its municipal bayside course in 1957 (in part to replace the Country Club's links). Among the prettiest courses in the country, it's one of dozens in San Diego County on which Hotel Del guests can play.

Activities Ongoing

The Del continued to keep up with the nation's sporting enthusiasms, adding options in response to guest preferences, including everything from water-skiing and surfing to beach volleyball and ocean-side yoga. In 2004, the hotel instituted its own beachfront ice-skating rink, open during the Christmas season.

FACING PAGE
Female bathers pose in the "plunge," c. 1915.

THIS PAGE TOP
The hotel's pier was used for strolling and fishing.

THIS PAGE MIDDLE LEFT
Note the weights of the fish written on the photograph, c. 1900.

THIS PAGE MIDDLE RIGHT
A group of hotel guests readies for a rabbit drive, c. 1900.

THIS PAGE BOTTOM RIGHT
A hunting party on North Island with The Del in the distant background, c. 1900.

FACING PAGE
Horses provided lots of entertainment for Hotel Del guests: beach "driving" (top), pony carts for the younger set (bottom left) and polo (bottom right).

#15- POLO- RANELAGH VS BRYN MAWR.
CORONADO CALIF. MARCH 20, 1909. H.R.FITCH PHOTO

Guests are cordially invited to attend a swimming
party in the hotel plunge

Wednesday evening at eight-thirty

to be followed by a moonlight weinie roast
on the beach

Please make reservations with the hostess

THIS PAGE
*Ocean bathers with the hotel's "plunge" in the background
(top); guests enjoying the plunge (left); a plunge party
invitation, possibly c. 1930 (bottom right).*

TOP LEFT AND TOP RIGHT
The hotel's present pool was constructed using old-fashioned horsepower (left), but when it debuted in 1934, it was a modern marvel (right).

MIDDLE LEFT
An acrobatic performance, c. 1934.

MIDDLE RIGHT
Canoeing in the pool, c. 1955.

BOTTOM RIGHT
A high-diving demonstration for ladies who lunch, c. 1956.

Let's
Go Sailing

at

Hotel del Coronado
Boat House
Coronado, California

For full details call the Boat House

SAILBOATS — OUTBOARD MOTORBOATS — ROWBOATS — CHARTERS — AQUAPLANING
WATERSKIING — SPORTFISHING — SAILING INSTRUCTION — SNACK BAR

THIS PAGE
*Counterclockwise from top: The hotel's original tennis court;
Simpson Sinsabaugh playing at the Coronado Country Club,
c. 1909; hotel tennis tournament, c. 1955; and champion
player – and frequent Del guest – Maureen Connolly in 1952.*

THIS PAGE

An early rendering of golf at The Del (top left); teeing off at the Coronado Country Club, c. 1915 (bottom left); a 1924 Country Club brochure specified house and golf rules (top right); the hotel's pitch-and-putt course, c. 1924 and c. 1950 (middle right); and the Coronado Municipal Golf Course debuts, c. 1960 (bottom right).

TENT LIFE AT CORONADO

BOAT HOUSE

By the Sea

In the Beginning

Under the direction of Del owner John D. Spreckels, Tent City was established in 1900 to appeal to America's emerging middle class. Located on land just south of the hotel, this camping alternative offered modest tent and bungalow accommodations to those who could not afford to stay in the "big hotel" — a clientele that hotel management diplomatically characterized as "those who, from choice, prefer camp life ... because of its novelty, its freedom and its attractions." Promoted as the "Sunset City of the Southwest, about a half-mile south of the Queen of all Hotels," Tent City "places the enjoyment within the reach of all," as its first brochure pointed out.

Situated on Coronado's Silver Strand between the Pacific Ocean and Glorietta Bay, Tent City was about 600 feet wide and grew to be a mile long, with more than 500 tents and cottages. Designed as a small city, its grid of dirt streets eventually became well-worn thoroughfares, lined with mature trees. Ultimately, Tent City sported restaurants and an ice cream parlor, library, grocery store, shops, a 40-room hotel (the Arcade), theater, bandstand, dance pavilion, merry-go-round, bowling alleys, shooting gallery, swimming floats (one with a high-diving board), police department and daily newspaper.

Tenting Accommodations

In a partnership with Santa Fe's Southern California Railway, Tent City offered its most favorable rates to those who came by train (and had a "return portion of a joint ticket" to prove it). In 1900, the smallest unfurnished tents, 8 by 10 feet, started at $1.50 per week (without a floor) and $2.50 per week (with floor), with reduced rates for extended stays. Visitors could also bring their own tents and pay a ground fee.

The largest unfurnished tent, 16 by 24 feet, was $7 a week, with floor. Furnishings were purchased à la carte: A single cot, table or oil lamp cost 25 cents per week, while a double bed with "spring and cotton mattress" was $1.25 a week. Furnished tents started at $3.50 per person per week and included a comfortable single or double bed, bedding, table, rocking and folding chairs, washstand, looking glass, mat on boarded floor, clean linen towels and lamp, as well as daily care of tent and laundry service.

In the Shadow of the Big Hotel

In 1900, even the most luxuriously appointed tent was a bargain compared to the cost of a hotel guestroom, which started around $3 per day. There was definitely a class distinction between hotel guests, who tended to have inherited wealth, and Tent City guests, who had to earn their livings. Still, there was a certain amount of social interaction between them, with Del guests enjoying a trek to Tent City for a concert or other special event and Tent City residents wandering over to the hotel to enjoy the gardens or a meal (breakfast and lunch cost 50 cents; dinner was 75 cents).

But the social divide between the two groups was real. In 1935, Paramount released the musical *Coronado*, the star-crossed story of a wealthy young hotel guest who falls in love with a poor Tent City singer.

Summer Season

Social standing was not the only difference between Tent City and the hotel. At that time, The Del's busy season was December through April, drawing winter vacationers from the cold midwestern and eastern states. Tent City's season was from June through September, attracting tourists from inland California, Arizona, Texas and New Mexico who wanted to escape the summer heat. Some Coronado residents also engaged tents as their own vacation getaways. Eventually Tent City evolved into a somewhat year-round resort, with permanent roofs replacing thatch, and included some year-round lease holders.

As with hotel visitors, many Tent City guests would stay for an entire summer season. Those of more modest means could enjoy an occasional afternoon outing, made all the more affordable by the rental bathing suits Tent City offered.

For Tent City season highlights, see page 146.

PREVIOUS PAGE
A Tent City brochure, c. 1900.

FACING PAGE
Tent City in its early days.

Coronado Tent City

DAILY PROGRAM

Vol. IV   CORONADO BEACH, CALIFORNIA, SATURDAY, AUGUST 22, 1903   No. 68

THE CORONADO TENT CITY DAILY PROGRAM is published daily at the Tent City and distributed freely for the information and amusement of the campers.

It is proper to state that, though the proprietors are interested in this publication in the same manner that they are interested in everything that pertains to the Tent City, they are in no sense responsible for the opinions or expressions of its editorial writer.

Correspondents having items for publication may leave them at the Tent City office or with the editor, George O. Jenner, at his tent, 1101½ Main street.

TEMPERATURE AT TENT CITY, AUGUST 21

Minimum thermometer....................... **70**
Maximum thermometer.................... **84**

TIDE TABLE, AUGUST 22.

HIGH TIDE :— 9:10 A. M.; 8:58 P. M.
LOW TIDE :— 2:50 A. M.; 2:49 P. M.

At the Cafe last evening Mr. Thill entertained a number of friends.

Mrs. Emerson H. Gruwell, of Riverside, is spending an outing at Coronado.

Mrs. J. C. Healy and family were dining at the Cafe on Wednesday evening.

Mr. an Mrs. Peter Becker, of San Diego, were dining at the restaurant on Wednesday evening.

Mrs. T A. Murray and family of Texas, with Miss Martha Jameson, of San Diego, reside at 1300.

A. H. Richardson, a prominent mining man of Kingman, Arizona, is visiting C. H. Burloch at Tent City.

Miss Hall, Miss Mote, Mr. Deemer and Mr. Sanborn formed a party for the theater on Amateur Night.

High ladies' scores at the Bowling Alleys include 139 by Miss Imply and 135 scored by Miss Chadwick.

Misses Bonnie and Vera Rockhold have returned to their home in Riverside after spending an outing at Coronado.

Musical Tent City has received an addition in the person of Mr. Martinez, one of the leading professors of Los Angeles.

Mr. Valle Paddock, of San Diego, gave a charming dinner party to a number of friends at the Cafe on Wednesday.

Mr. and Mrs. Williams, Miss Mabel Williams, and Mrs. Evans spent the week end at the Mikado tent on Twenty-second street.

CHURCH NOTICES.

The services at Christ Episcopal Church on Sunday are the Sunday-school at 9:45 and morning prayer and sermon at 11 Evening service in the auditorium of Tent City at 7:45. Rev. Charles E. Spalding, rector. Walk to C avenue or take car to Ninth street. Mr. Spalding will preach at the morning service on the subject of "Faith and Service."

A bright, interesting Sunday-school is held at the Pavilion every Sunday at 9:45. Children and their parents are earnestly invited to attend.

Sunday-school at the Pavilion tomorrow at 9:45. Singing and addresses. All children are invited. Mr. and Mrs. Cameron in charge. At 7:45 Rev. Charles Spalding will conduct services at the theatre. Special music under the direction of Prof. Leon Stanton. The augmented choir will sing Gounod's "Sanctus."

Graham Memorial Presbyterian Church, Coronado, Sunday evening, August 23. Sermon: "Living Positively," by Rev. Luther Davis. Mrs. U. F. Newlin will sing Stainer's "My Hope is in the Everlasting." Services commence at 11 o'clock.

POPCORN THURSDAY.

To attempt a description of children's day would be mere folly, for such joy as prevailed on Thursday could never be boiled down to cold type. Sufficient it is to say that Mrs. Lyon eclipsed all her previous efforts along this line, and the last celebration will mark an epoch in the lives of many of our young guests. The popcorn proved a great drawing card, and a little over 300 sacks were distributed. The parade with "Cash's" band at the head brought all the camp down on Main street, and the scene was an extremely brilliant one as the procession of merry faces wended its way to the spot where Mrs. Deemer and Mrs. Lyon presided over a mountain of popcorn.

There was the usual dance on the Casino of course, and some entertainment in the way of singing. Little Ernest Martinez, a 6-year-old youngster from Los Angeles, delightfully sang numbers from "Il Trovatore," and in order to display his remarkable versatility switched off into "Ain't that a Shame" with the greatest possible ease. Truly a great day for the children.

Mr. Wood, the secretary of the San Diego Chamber of Commerce, dined with his family at the Tent City restaurant on Wednesday.

EXCURSIONS THURSDAY.

To the Japanese Tea Garden by automobile:
  Mesdames Hardy, Hill, Cummings, Andrews, E. F. Chandler, H. E. Mulford, and Madeline and Chester Mulford.
To Tia Juana by tally-ho:
  Mr. Ballentyne and wife, J. S. Quinn, J. Blum, Mr. Prince.
To Point Loma by tally-ho:
  H. B. Hackett, wife and children, P. H. Hawkins and wife, Mrs. Whipp, Misses Whipp.

A private driving party to Tia Juana included Mr. and Mrs. Taylor, Mr. Heywood, Jr., Mrs. Heywood and Mrs. Moorhead.

Mrs. Rehooldt (Mr. Bennett's mother-in-law ! !) entertained at dinner on Thursday evening Miss Moore and Fred Chanter.

Mrs. La Badie, Mrs. J. E. Shields, Miss Elsie Shields, and Miss Ivy Ramsbottom, of Riverside, are enjoying a summer outing at Tent City.

Mrs. Irwin entertained a party of four friends at the Cafe on Wednesday evening, previous to enjoying the evening's pleasures at the resort.

Mrs. Lyon's dancing class for children will be held on the Casino at 2:30 this afternoon. Mrs. Lyon is an instructor with an enviable reputation.

There is no necessity to go to the big cities for a first class vaudeville performance. At the Pavilion Theatre the best of talent hold forth every night.

At the Amusement Parlors the Manhattan competition is attracting a deal of attention. Mr. George Carter is still in the lead for the prize, with a score of 1370.

BENDIX—On Wednesday evening next from the band stand will be played a program of music made up entirely from the masterly compositions of Bendix.

Mr. E. Lake, a former secretary of the San Diego Chamber of Commerce and native of Colorado, was attending the picnic gathering of people from his native state on Friday.

The children are certainly getting $3,000 worth of fun out of that bathing pool. From early morn till late in the afternoon it seems that the number ever increases. The water is at a temperature just suited to the young ones, and with the sunshine and other favorable conditions here is a remarkable health provider.

4319. View of Tent City, looking toward Hotel Coronado. Coronado, Cal.

Coronado Tent City — Looking Southeast.

FACING PAGE

The daily newspaper, Coronado Tent City, *was an ambitious undertaking, eight pages in length, which listed guest arrivals and activities, local attractions, the day's band program and dozens of display ads for Tent City, Coronado and San Diego businesses.*

THIS PAGE TOP LEFT AND TOP RIGHT

Two early postcards showed the center thoroughfare (left) and the ocean-side boardwalk (right), which featured this imprinted text on the reverse side: "As a place of rest, recuperation and recreation from the noise and bustle of metropolitan life, a week's vacation at Tent City is one of the most novel, unique and entertaining of anywhere on the western coast."

THIS PAGE ABOVE AND RIGHT

A Tent City brochure showcased a well-appointed tent (above) and the Tent City Café (right).

THIS PAGE
A trio of early Tent City photos includes the children's pool in 1905 (top), which a brochure described as "the children's greatest delight … the scene of the liveliest fun and jollity."
The brochure continued, "All this fun and merriment is absolutely free to those who bring their own bathing suits, and those who do not can rent suits at low rates at Bath House No. 2, close by this great joy-giving pool."

TOP
*Children of visiting Pittsburgh Orchestra members
enjoyed a cool Tent City outing in 1906.*

BOTTOM LEFT
Tent City's 1906 Fourth of July celebration.

BOTTOM RIGHT
*Professional photographer William D. Zimmerman took
this photograph of himself with wife Olive in 1905.*

13862 PAVILION AND WALK, CORONADO TENT CITY, CALIF.

LEFT

The Tent City Band (top left) gave concerts in the bayside dance pavilion (middle left), reportedly one of the largest facilities of its kind on the West Coast when it opened in 1910. The group on the beach (bottom left) may have been vaudeville performers.

ABOVE

These two snapshots are from the scrapbook of Malcolm Robinson, manager of Tent City, c. 1911–1917.

GRAND PATRIOTIC PAGEANT
at Coronado Tent City
Sunday, September 8

The 32nd Regiment Band from Camp Kearny Will Present
an All Day Program of

OLD TIME SPORTS

Rowing and Swimming Races, Sack and Potato Races, Jumping and
High Diving, Three-Legged Races, etc., etc.

PLENTY OF GOOD MUSIC

AUGUST 31 TO SEPTEMBER 6, 1918

CORONADO
TENT CITY NEWS

OFFICIAL PROGRAM

Conserve—Do Not Throw This Program Away—Conserve

THIS PAGE

*World War I at Tent City: Patriotic guests outfitted their tent with
American flags in 1918 (top left); five-year-old Alfreda Smith
performed with a military band on September 16, 1917 (top
right); and a program urged wartime visitors to conserve (bottom
right) and boasted a "Grand Patriotic Pageant" (above).*

Season Highlights

1900: Although the number of visitors might have been exaggerated (in newspapers and by the hotel itself), it was estimated that 10,000 people attended the 1900 Fourth of July celebration.

1904 Brochure: By this time, 13 "palm cottages" had been added, all facing the ocean, utilizing 1,000 ripe palm leaves in the construction of each roof and "very suggestive of an ancient Moorish village." At 18 by 22 feet, these could accommodate up to five people, with curtains to divide the cottage into separate sleeping areas. Also included in the brochure was this short poem written by a Pomona College student: *Quarter, ticket, trolley, girl / music, actors, dancers, whirl / moonlight evenings, breakers, kiss / Coronado — perfect bliss.*

1910 *Tent City News*: An "Official Program" included the announcement that former White House Chef Louis Bozin (under President Cleveland) "presides over the culinary department of the Tent City Café ... one of the most noted chefs ever brought to America [from Paris]."

1911/1912 Brochures: From 1911: "Owing to the entire absence of rowdyism, sometimes found at watering places, mothers can leave their children here to romp at will, in perfect assurance that no harm can befall them." A 1912 brochure touted the benefits of Tent City's "open air": "It means robust children when school bells ring again in the fall. It prolongs life and enables the accomplishment of more work, with less effort."

1918 Brochure: With America's entry into World War I, the 1918 Tent City pamphlet was modest in size and began by promoting its proximity to San Diego's Fort Rosecrans and the "Government Aviation Headquarters" in Coronado, "The aeroplanes in flight being unceasing objects of interest to Tent City's population."

1918 *Tent City News*, August 31 to September 6: In support of the war effort, the cover of this 30-page publication cautioned Tent City visitors to "Conserve — Do Not Throw This Program Away — Conserve." Much of the program was given over to wartime news, including a report on funds raised for "the Salvation Army work on the battlefields of Europe." A grand military ball was planned for September 14, with announcements to "Buy thrift stamps now." On a much lighter note, there was a listing of "fanciful names" given to Tent City's "temporary domiciles" that were characterized as "odd and interesting appellations bestowed by campers," including Call Inn, Due Drop Inn, Waldorf-Astoria Inn, Camp Contentment Inn, Seldom Inn, Wobble Inn and We're Inn.

1924 Brochure: By 1924, a special note for motorists informed them they could "park their machines near their tent houses or cottages free of charge, though low rates prevail at a well-equipped garage at one end of the resort." Palm Cottages were now all equipped with toilets and running water, some with baths, and there was a new addition: public telephone booths.

1925 Hotel Del Menu: A June 5, 1925, dinner menu for the Crown Room included this tribute to Tent City's 25th summer season: "A resort of over 500 cozy palm cottages, tent houses and beach bungalows, Tent City is the vacation place each year for summer sojourners. An additional attraction this year will be free moving pictures every evening with orchestral music ... given in the large open-air pavilion."

1928 Brochure: By 1928, Tent City's brochure had expanded in size and featured a wonderful bird's-eye drawing, complete with a biplane soaring overhead. Despite some new accommodations and modernizations, Tent City crowds had begun to thin, in part due to waning interest in camping vacations nationwide. With the 1926 death of John D. Spreckels — who some say had been financially underwriting Tent City every year since 1900 — the future of Tent City was precarious.

1935 Brochure: Thanks to San Diego's 1935 California-Pacific International Exposition, many visitors spilled over into Tent City, which had begun promoting its year-round accommodations: "Coronado's climate is featured by cool summers and balmy winters." The Great Depression was now in full swing, and Tent City addressed it admirably: "Consistent with the trend of the times, rates provide a maximum of healthful and invigorating vacation for a surprisingly nominal sum." Despite the Depression, housing at Tent City was more diversified than ever with the addition of new cabins (including garages) and deluxe cottages, "recently completed and consisting of combination living room and dining room."

The End of an Era

Even with The Del's best efforts to keep Tent City both modern and affordable, by the late 1930s, the Depression had taken its toll. In addition, Coronado's Navy base, with war brewing in Europe, wanted to widen the Strand road (which Tent City impeded) for improved and speedier accessibility to North Island. Tent City celebrated its last season in 1938.

Although Tent City was dismantled, some of its buildings were recycled (a further reflection of the nation's tough economic times): Roof trusses from the dancing pavilion were used in the construction of the movie theater at North Island; the former merry-go-round ended up at the entrance to the San Diego Zoo; and many of the bungalows were sold and then moved intact to other locations, leading to the speculation that remnants of Tent City cottages probably still exist in Coronado.

THIS PAGE
Tent City bathing beauties (top) and Tent City brochures from the 1930s (bottom).

From Near and Far

Conventioneers

The First Conventions

The first convention for which the hotel has records is the Hotel Men's Mutual Benefit Association, held at The Del on April 21, 1896. According to an article in the *New York Times*, the president of the group spoke, praising Southern California's incomparable climate:

We who come from the cold, effete and clammy East, with as we are with pride and codfish, pie and self-esteem, have been touched and electrified by the kindness and courtesies which have been so prodigally bestowed upon us from the moment we entered the portals of this lovely land of sunshine and flowers. This languorous climate suits me. I'd like to get not too arduous occupation out here, like picking blossoms off a century plant.

A few years later, a meeting of the Southern California Editorial Association was reported at Tent City: "The members of the Association have come to town and settled at Camp Content, and everybody bids them welcome. The peninsula is theirs, the town is theirs, the sea and ocean round about is at their disposal."

A program from a 1913 California Bar Association meeting also took a lighthearted tone with its "Writ of Attendance":

We command you all and singular, business and excuses set aside, that you appear and attend a banquet given in your honor at Hotel del Coronado, and then there you shall eat to your satiety; you shall drink consistent with sobriety; you shall consume all the joy your capacity may hold, and finally, that you shall in peace and quiet listen to the oratory which will be suitably provided for the occasion.

By the 1920s, a wide range of groups were meeting at the hotel (many with repeat visits), including California Western States Life Insurance Company, State Federation of Women's Clubs, Santa Fe Loss and Damage Prevention, American Association of Railway Advertisers, California Medical Association and Delta Gamma Sorority.

Meeting Rooms

In the early days, the hotel's Ballroom was the only large meeting room. By 1931, convention demand had outpaced the room's size, and it was undergoing "extensive alterations ... which will give the famous hostelry the largest convention auditorium of any resort hotel west of Chicago."

Plans included an extension of 15 feet on three sides "elevated above the dance floor, permitting an unobstructed view of the stage." The extension gave the hotel the capacity to accommodate general sessions of large state, Pacific Coast, western and national organizations.

Into the Modern Meeting Era

When the Western Confectioners met at The Del in 1932, they issued an irresistible invitation in their "Ice Cream News."

Four days at the beautiful Hotel del Coronado — three mornings of serious business discussion and four afternoons of delightful recreation, besides the inevitable annual golf tournament, are the prospects facing the members ... once before the confectioners met at Coronado and those who attended that convention have since been unable to forget the enjoyable time spent there.

By 1940, the hotel was also promoting air transportation (mostly between Los Angeles and San Diego), drawing attention to the "luxury ships" offered by Western Air, United and American Airlines.

Although the Great Depression and World War II must have put a damper on convention activities, by the 1950s, more lobby-level area was given over to meeting rooms. By 1960, some additional interior modifications were being made to the hotel, in part to capture increased meeting and banquet business, as conventions became an important economic component of the American travel industry, generating hotel and airline revenue as well as a host of related businesses.

With the completion of the Coronado Bridge in 1969, as well as the construction of Grande Hall in 1973 (a contemporary conference facility) and California Cabanas in 1979 (providing additional breakout meeting rooms), the Hotel del Coronado continued to keep pace with convention demand.

PREVIOUS PAGE
A c. 1925 convention group poses on The Del's steps.

FACING PAGE
Many mid-century conventions arranged for formal photos of all attendees; however, this picture, c. 1950, captures an informal crowd of guests — perhaps readying for a special event — during a Retail Grocers Convention.

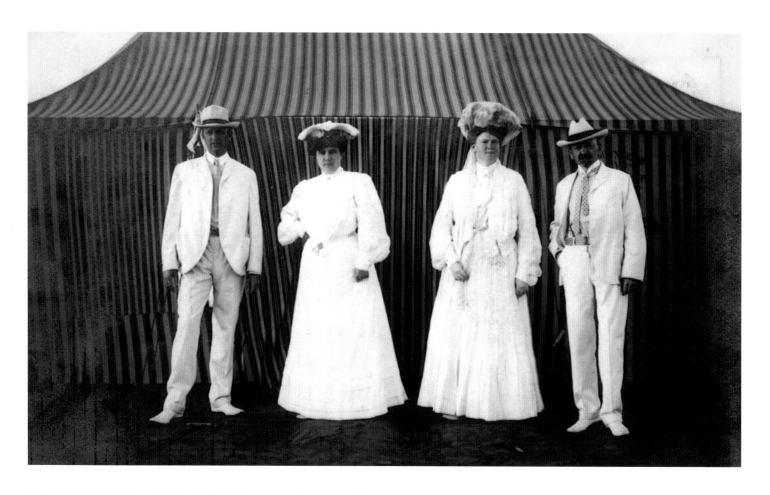

THIS PAGE TOP

Dr. and Mrs. Colleschon, along with Dr. and Mrs. Richard Berndt, attended a medical convention at The Del, c. 1905. They might have stayed in Tent City, given the striped tent in the background; the doctors were recent Berkeley graduates.

THIS PAGE LEFT

The 1920 California Retail Shoe Dealers' Association program was 12 pages in length and featured daily programs.

FACING PAGE TOP

A c. 1932 convention brochure featured a photo of the Ballroom and spoke to The Del's technical capabilities, which included a "loud speaker system," along with "the latest Western Electric Sound Equipment for talking pictures."

FACING PAGE BOTTOM

A handcrafted note was received by The Del in thanks for a 1938 Lincoln National Life Insurance meeting.

The famous Ball Room of Hotel del Coronado, where presidents, princes, international delegations and notables from throughout the world have been entertained. Admirably suited for convention purposes.

To Hotel del Coronado

In acknowledgment of the splendid cooperation extended us during our

Western Regional Convention

June 22, 23, 24, 1938.

The Lincoln National Life Insurance Company

Fort Wayne, Indiana

A. L. Sm
Vice President

Hotel Conventions Circa 1932

Conventions were held at the Hotel del Coronado from its beginning days, but this c. 1932 sales brochure (cover above) is the earliest in the resort's archives. Although it included many photos and some typeset design elements and text, most of the brochure was typed on Del stationery. The brochure cover featured the title "Hotel del Coronado, Coronado Beach, California: Ideal Spot for Conventions" and drew special attention to the hotel's entertainment capabilities:

> The variety of entertainment offered to delegates of conventions and placed at their disposal assists the Entertainment Committee in planning their program, creating a feeling of good fellowship, so that the pleasant memories carried away of an enjoyable time spent at Hotel del Coronado linger long after the more serious matters of the convention are forgotten.

The kinds of entertainment listed included boat rides; bridge parties (table prizes provided by the hotel); weekly dances; golf tournaments at the Coronado Country Club; talking pictures; swimming ("still-water bathing in hotel plunge, filled with warmed and filtered seawater"); horseback riding ("excellent mounts may be secured from the Country Club stables"); and tennis (one hotel court; two Country Club courts).

Rates during this Depression-era period were "the lowest we have offered to conventions in years and have been adjusted in keeping with the times," starting at $7 for a single room with bathroom, $6 without. Meals for nonregistered guests were $1.50 per person for breakfast and lunch, $2 for dinner (Room Service was an additional charge of 50 cents per person).

Of course, Coronado's wonderful weather and its proximity to San Diego sightseeing was also touted.

ORDINARY AGENCIES WESTERN

CONFERENCE

1953

Hotel del Coronado is built around a brilliant California garden. Your group deserves this perfect setting.

THIS PAGE TOP
A retrospective of the 1953 Prudential Life Insurance Company conference showcased some of The Del's many amenities.

THIS PAGE LEFT
A c. 1955 brochure featured a full-color rendering of a lobby-level area.

FACING PAGE TOP
Federal Life Insurance convention, c. 1955.

FACING PAGE BOTTOM LEFT
After World War II, the hotel emphasized its "house party" atmosphere in a c. 1948 convention brochure.

FACING PAGE BOTTOM RIGHT
By the end of the 1950s, conventions at the Hotel del Coronado were in full swing.

FEDERAL LIFE INSURANCE COMPANY
37th MEETING — CONVENTION CLUB

―――― Hotel del Coronado ――――

Coronado . . .

Hotel del Coronado is the ideal place for your convention. Without exception, commercial and social organizations have highly commended the Hotel upon its location, convention facilities and its "on the spot" recreational facilities.

The fact that delegates live, meet, dine and have their swimming, tennis, sailing or restful sun-lazing all in one delightful place provides elements of fellowship and friendliness that contribute greatly to the convention's success.

Your convention can enjoy the "house-party" spirit that prevails at Coronado, where full participation in the convention program is the logical, easy thing to do.

―――― Both The Sunshine and The Sea ――――

PIONEER

Pioneer American Insurance Company - Fort Worth, Texas

Hotel del Coronado

WELCOME PIONEER AMERICAN INS CO

PIONEER AMERICAN'S
One Hundred Million Dollar
STATESIDE CONVENTION
ISSUE

APRIL 1959

THIS PAGE AND FACING PAGE
*During the 1950s and 1960s, a hotel photographer
regularly recorded convention events, including a hat-making
contest (facing page, top right) and a dance line during a
Dairy & Poultry Association event (this page, bottom left).*

Outdoor Party and Reception Facilities

Certainly one of the major attractions for group activities at Hotel del Coronado is the wonderful range of outdoor party facilities. You may plan to enjoy these events with confidence in the pleasant Coronado weather, too. The Hotel's broad acres of white sand beach provide an appetite-whetting setting for steak fries, barbecues and picnics that can add greatly to the enjoyment of your convention.

Western Plastics

JUNE 1970

REPORT ON CORONADO: WESTERNERS MOLD
PROGRAM FOR THE SEVENTIES

THE ONLY LARGE OCEAN FRONT RESORT HOTEL ON THE WEST COAST

FACING PAGE
A c. 1967 convention brochure included a photo of a large poolside luncheon.

THIS PAGE TOP LEFT
In June 1970, Western Plastics featured the Garden Patio on the cover of its industry newsletter.

THIS PAGE TOP RIGHT AND BOTTOM RIGHT
By the mid-1970s, the resort's convention brochure featured a photo with the Coronado Bridge in the background and the newly constructed Ocean Towers in the foreground (top). The brochure also showcased the resort's recreational amenities, including the "Turquoise Pool," which still featured a high-diving board (bottom).

FACING PAGE

In 1993, The Del held its largest event to date — a party for the National Conference of State Legislators, with 4,500 in attendance.

THIS PAGE TOP

During the 1994 Pillsbury Bake-Off, Grande Hall was outfitted with 100 mini-kitchens.

THIS PAGE RIGHT

Conventions at the Hotel del Coronado were state-of-the-art in the 1990s, but available technology seems vintage by today's standards, as this c. 1994 Business Center brochure illustrates.

The Business Center offers:

Copying
Clean, professional copies at 15 cents per page, including collating and stapling. Volume discounts are available. Overhead transparencies are $3.00 per page.

Facsimile Transmission
Fast, accurate communications - around the world. To send a domestic FAX is $5.00 for the first page and $3.00 for each additional page. To send an international FAX is $10.00 for the first page and $6.00 for each additional page. To receive any FAX is $1.00 per page.

Typing and Word Processing
With advance notice, professional typing, word processing and dictation service is available at $10.00 per page.

Mail Packages Service
Stamps, envelopes, boxes, packing materials and tape are available. There is a handling charge of $5.00 for shipment of packages.

Communications rentals, too.

Pagers
Numeric and Alphanumeric pagers with county-wide coverage, $15.00 per day.

Radio
Walkie-talkie for two-way communications, $25.00 each per day, $100.00 each per week.

Typewriter
$8.00 per hour, $20.00 per day, or $50 per week.

Dictaphone Recorder
$10.00 per day.

Cellular Phone
Pocket cellular phones are available at $15.00 per day, plus airtime charges.

Personal Computer
$10.00 per hour, $70.00 per day.

On the Guest Register

A Presidential Roster

The Hotel del Coronado's presidential history dates to **President Benjamin Harrison (1889–1893)**, who was touring the country by train. This was the first time an in-office president had visited San Diego. Reportedly, Harrison greeted San Diego well-wishers in his dressing robe and slippers from the back of his railcar. On April 23, 1891, Harrison had breakfast at The Del. When he left Coronado, Harrison received a sendoff at the ferry slip, serenaded by the Coronado Band, which a local newspaper reported could "vie with any band in the country in discoursing good music." Later Harrison told future President William Taft (another Del visitor), "One who has ever breathed this atmosphere would want to live here always."

President William Taft (1909–1913) had a sister living in Coronado, whom he visited in April 1900. After his presidency, Taft stayed at The Del to attend the 1915 Panama-California Exposition.

President Franklin Roosevelt (1933–1945) visited The Del for the first time in 1914, when he was Assistant Secretary of the Navy and made the trip to assess San Diego's harbor and nearby North Island. He also attended San Diego's 1915 exposition. President Roosevelt returned again in 1935 with Mrs. Roosevelt for San Diego's California-Pacific International Exposition, where he gave a speech to 50,000 people in Balboa Park. During his stay, Roosevelt flew the presidential flag from The Del's turret, making the hotel the official White House during his stay.

Former **President Lyndon Johnson (1963–1969)** attended President Nixon's 1970 state dinner for Mexico's president, Gustavo Díaz Ordaz.

On September 3, 1970, **President Richard Nixon (1969–1974)** hosted a state dinner in the Crown Room for Mexico's president, Gustavo Díaz Ordaz. Among the 1,000 people in attendance were former President and Mrs. Lyndon Johnson and California Governor and Mrs. Ronald Reagan. Aside from political luminaries, the dinner was also attended by Hollywood celebrities such as Frank Sinatra and John Wayne.

President Gerald Ford (1974–1977) attended an economic conference at The Del in April 1975. He made other visits to the hotel in 1980, 1991, 1992 and 1993.

When **President Jimmy Carter (1977–1981)** attended the AFL-CIO Building and Construction Trades convention in 1979, a Del reception was given in his honor on October 11. Carter also stayed at the hotel in 1989 in conjunction with a Habitat for Humanity project; he and Mrs. Carter made a more recent visit in 2012.

After attending Nixon's state dinner in 1970, **President Ronald Reagan (1981–1989)** returned to The Del on October 8, 1982, when he hosted talks with Mexico's president-elect, Miguel de la

Madrid. Reagan had a long history with The Del, beginning in the late 1940s, when he worked as an actor in Hollywood. Later visits included family vacations in the 1960s, and as California governor, Reagan attended the Coronado Bridge dedication in 1969.

President George H. Bush (1989–1993), an avid tennis player, enjoyed staying at the hotel before and during his presidency.

President Bill Clinton (1993–2001), along with wife Hillary and daughter Chelsea, vacationed frequently at The Del during his presidency. In Coronado, Clinton played golf; Chelsea took tennis lessons; and the entire family enjoyed biking the city's streets.

President George W. Bush (2001–2005) stayed at The Del in August 2005 while attending a 60th anniversary celebration of V-J Day at North Island.

Continued on page 166

Presidential Preparations

The most detailed description of what is required for a presidential visit is contained in hotel files from President Reagan's 1982 meeting with another head of state, President-elect de la Madrid of Mexico.

The day before, all cars were cleared from the back parking lot, bomb teams started arriving, and security staff for Reagan and de la Madrid were assigned guestrooms (numbering around 100).

By the time Reagan and de la Madrid arrived, the back exterior staircase had been equipped with a ramp, the entire area was curtained off for security, and a nearby elevator was put out of service. Additional draping was provided along the first, second and third floor exterior hallways. The lobby mezzanine was also curtained off, and staircase access was limited. Certain offices were vacated and secured, as were some closets. The windows in the Coronet Room were covered in Mylar and draped.

The group's departure — from a doorway in the Coronet Room — required even more extensive preparations. The area was curtained off, and a ramp was installed (according to specifications: "must be gradual and must hold 12,000 pounds"). The ramp connected the front entrance to the valet parking lot, requiring the removal of a hedge for motorcade access. The media was not allowed to cover Reagan's arrival or departure.

RIGHT
President Franklin Roosevelt (in the back seat at left) arriving at The Del in 1935, accompanied by the governor of California, Frank Merriam (to F.D.R.'s left).

F.D.R. at The Del

Roosevelt had close ties to Coronado from his days as Woodrow Wilson's Assistant Secretary of the Navy, when he befriended G. Aubrey Davidson, a leading San Diego businessman who resided full time at The Del. They first met in 1914, when Roosevelt arrived to survey the harbor; he returned in 1915 for the Panama-California Exposition, deeming the harbor — with improved access provided by the newly completed Panama Canal — an ideal location for "the reception of the world's navies."

1935

Roosevelt returned to The Del in 1935 for another Balboa Park exposition. As reported by the November issue of *California Life*, after traveling by ferry across the bay, President and Mrs. Roosevelt arrived at the Hotel del Coronado on October 1, 1935, accompanied by "whistles blowing from the time the presidential party left the ferry until they came through the private entrance, lined on either side by Marines."

The couple entered through the "back" of the hotel, "with hundreds of blue-coated, white-capped Marines with fixed bayonets scattered throughout the tropical garden." After being met by a large welcoming committee, the president and first lady "dined quietly in their apartment." Later that evening, Mrs. Roosevelt enjoyed a swim in the "Turquoise Pool," which had been "reserved for their exclusive use."

Presidential Accommodations

The "Presidential Suite" was located on the ocean side of the hotel and featured a large reception hall, dining room and two living rooms; a spacious ocean-facing porch rounded out the accommodations. A local newspaper reported, "The chief executive enjoyed an inspiring view of the broad Pacific, where a goodly part of the United States fleet rode at anchor, the lights from the warships shedding their glow over the temporary White House."

The warships must have been impressive, as reported in the *San Diego Union* on October 2, 1935: "President Roosevelt slept un-der the guns of the entire United States fleet at Hotel del Coronado last night." Another article also stressed the presence of the United States Navy: "The lights of the fleet ... bathed the temporary White House in a flood of brilliance, as Marine guards patrolled the hotel property and drew a close cordon around the presidential suite."

Another article added: "The military represented the pomp and circumstance and care with which the country surrounds its First Citizen, [but] Mr. and Mrs. Roosevelt, at ease in lounging chairs in their suite, were to outside appearances just two American citizens on a tour."

While President Roosevelt's suite was described as "masculine in spirit, with walnut brown furniture and ivory and brown tones throughout," Mrs. Roosevelt's accommodations were "in soft green and ivory ... a quiet and delightful retreat where she was able to relax from the day's heavy program ... her own sitting room appointed appropriately in ivory and Eleanor blue." Reportedly, Mrs. Roosevelt was so taken with the beauty of the hotel that she asked an accompanying doctor if he "could not find something the matter with her so she could remain longer."

Official Business

In addition to the Roosevelts' quarters, an additional 65 guestrooms were engaged for the presidential party, which included a variety of government and military officials, including Secretary of the Interior Harold Ickes, Kentucky Senator A.W. Barkley (later President Truman's vice president), and William H. Moran, chief of the Secret Service.

During F.D.R.'s visit, the presidential flag flew from an exterior hotel turret and also marked the entrance to the presidential suite. Special phone and telegraph lines were installed with direct access to Washington, and a press room was set up to "speed messages to the leading press associations." In Coronado only for a couple of days, Roosevelt also met with the Infantile Paralysis Association before attending the Balboa Park exposition.

As a footnote: President and Mrs. Roosevelt were frequent Coronado guests during World War II, in part because their sons were sometimes stationed nearby.

ABOVE LEFT
President and Mrs. Franklin Roosevelt during their 1935 visit.

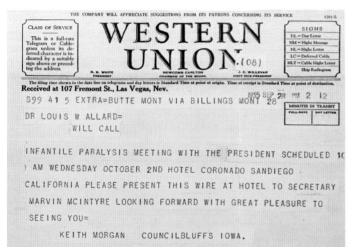

PRESIDENT FRANKLIN D. ROOSEVELT
AND MRS. ROOSEVELT

Pictured in their suite at Hotel del Coronado, the temporary White House, during their recent sojourn there early in October.

—Harold Taylor Photograph

TOP LEFT
President Roosevelt during his San Diego speech.

TOP RIGHT
President and Mrs. Roosevelt were photographed in their Hotel Del suite.

BOTTOM LEFT
A telegram confirmed President Roosevelt's Infantile Paralysis Association meeting.

BOTTOM RIGHT
The woman seated with Mrs. Roosevelt is Rose Harbin Davidson, wife of G. Aubrey Davidson, who conceived the 1935 exposition and oversaw much of its operations. The Davidsons, who resided at The Del for a couple of decades, forged a personal friendship with President and Mrs. Roosevelt.

ABOVE

In 1970, President Richard Nixon's motorcade en route to the Hotel del Coronado, with President Gustavo Díaz Ordaz of Mexico, drew throngs of well-wishers and media.

LEFT

When President Richard Nixon entertained Mexico's president, Gustavo Díaz Ordaz, the dinner in the Crown Room included a sea bass appetizer, along with prime sirloin Mexicana and bombe Guadalupe. The head table hosted (left to right) former First Lady Mrs. Lyndon Johnson; California Governor Ronald Reagan, First Lady Mrs. Richard Nixon; Mexico President Díaz Ordaz; President Nixon; President Ordaz's daughter; Mrs. Ronald Reagan and former President Lyndon Johnson.

TOP LEFT AND TOP RIGHT
President and Mrs. Carter spoke about their work with Habitat for Humanity in 1989 (left). In an earlier visit in 1979, President Carter greeted the hotel's culinary staff (right).

BOTTOM RIGHT
President Gerald Ford, who retired to Palm Springs after his presidency, made frequent visits to The Del, this one in 1980.

THIS PAGE

Ronald Reagan said he made the decision to ask Nancy to marry him during a visit to The Del, where she was on hand to hear a speech he gave at a Junior League convention. The couple is shown here at The Del, c. 1965 (top left). As governor of California, Reagan officiated at the 1969 opening of the Coronado Bridge, after which he attended a luncheon in the Crown Room (middle left). Before meeting with President-elect de la Madrid of Mexico in 1982, Reagan enjoyed talking with his supporters at The Del (bottom left).

In 1983, George H. Bush spoke at the hotel during his vice presidency (top right); he also enjoyed a game of tennis (bottom right).

THIS PAGE
Although Dwight Eisenhower was the first president to land at Coronado's Naval Air Station, President Bill Clinton used the airfield many times during his numerous visits to The Del (arriving on Air Force One). Clinton also enjoyed greeting supporters in the Garden Patio; golfing in Coronado; and strolling the grounds with Mrs. Clinton, who sported a Hotel Del cap.

It Started with Silent Films

Since the early 1900s movie stars and moviemakers have been frequenting the Hotel del Coronado, a sought-after set for filmmakers as well as a popular vacation getaway for celebrities. The first movie filmed at The Del was a short, silent documentary called *Off for the Rabbit Chase*, produced by the Edison Moving Picture Company in 1898. A handful of similar films followed, including one titled *Ferryboat Entering Slip* (c. 1901).

The first feature film made at the hotel was *Maiden and Men* (1912), a romance set at a posh resort, which *Motion Picture World* characterized as "a bewildering array of settings whose equal have certainly never before been seen in motion pictures." Other movies followed, including *Miss Jackie of the Navy* (1916), in which the hotel's courtyard was cast as a South Sea island.

Rudolph Valentino made two films at The Del: *The Married Virgin* (1918) and *Beyond the Rocks* (1922) with Gloria Swanson. (*The Married Virgin*, now available on DVD, has wonderful footage of The Del, its gardens and the beach.) Swanson returned to Coronado to play a young heiress in *Coast of Folly* (1925), one in a series of movies that helped establish the hotel as a beautiful backdrop for storylines that involved characters of wealth and privilege.

On to Talkies

The 1929 "talkie" *The Flying Fleet*, the story of two Navy aviators competing for one woman's affection, brought romance to its star, Anita Page. She fell in love with a local Navy officer, married him and eventually settled in Coronado and raised two daughters. Page was extremely popular in her day, said to be second only to Greta Garbo in the amount of fan mail received.

A high point in the Hotel Del's filmography was the movie musical *Coronado* (1935), starring Johnny Downs, a young man who had grown up in Coronado and appeared in *Our Gang* comedies. In the story of a rich hotel kid who falls in love with a Tent City chanteuse, Downs tap-danced atop The Del's mahogany bar. The film also featured Jack Haley, Andy Devine and the Eddy Duchin Orchestra. Another Depression-era film made at The Del was *Yours for the Asking* (1936), which starred George Raft, Dolores Costello and Ida Lupino.

Continued on page 176

RIGHT
This photo is thought to have been taken during the filming of **The Pearl of Paradise** *(1916), starring Margarita Fischer.*

Modern Moviemaking

Some Like It Hot — the movie most associated with The Del — was filmed in September 1958 (released in 1959), starring Marilyn Monroe, Tony Curtis and Jack Lemmon (see pages 182-187).

Years later, the slick crime caper *$* (1971), directed by Richard Brooks and starring Goldie Hawn and Warren Beatty, included a climactic rendezvous at The Del. *Loving Couples* (1980), with Shirley MacLaine, James Coburn, Susan Sarandon and Stephen Collins, recast the hotel as the "Delmonico Lodge," the setting for a double tryst, and included wonderful shots of the lobby, elevator, porte cochere and Garden Patio (recast as a restaurant).

The Stunt Man (filmed at The Del in 1977–78, but not released until 1980) tells the story of a maniacal movie director, played by Peter O'Toole, who allows a fugitive to work as a stuntman in his World War I-era film, almost killing him in the process. The movie includes dramatic scenes atop The Del's roof, where a fake tower was constructed and then blown up.

The End of an Era

By the 1970s, it had become increasingly difficult to accommodate moviemaking requests, as film crews grew larger and filming took longer and was more intrusive. However, a few memorable movie scenes were filmed at The Del in the '80s and '90s.

Jim Belushi — along with his canine costar — enjoyed a meal at the hotel's oceanfront restaurant in the 1989 movie *K-9*. In *My Blue Heaven* (1990), starring Steve Martin, Joan Cusack and Rick Moranis, there's a delightful dance scene on the Sun Deck, with a romantic dinner for two on the beach. And in 1995, Ellen DeGeneres and Bill Pullman shot a couple of scenes in the Ballroom and poolside for the movie *Mr. Wrong*, which was released in 1996.

A number of television episodes were also shot at The Del for shows such as *Baywatch*, *Hart to Hart* and *Simon & Simon*.

Celebrity Vacationers

Aside from its moviemaking celebrity roster, the Hotel del Coronado has been a vacation destination for Hollywood stars since its earliest days, with visitors such as W.C. Fields, Douglas Fairbanks and Charlie Chaplin. Later years brought a steady stream of Hollywood royalty, including Mary Pickford (who filmed *A Girl of Yesterday* at North Island), Al Jolson, the Marx Brothers, Greta Garbo, Mae West, John Barrymore, Rita Hayworth, Gary Cooper, Edward G. Robinson, Joan Crawford, Anthony Quinn, Jimmy Stewart, Judy Garland, Mickey Rooney, Katharine Hepburn, Gregory Peck, Charleton Heston, Maureen O'Hara, Kirk Douglas, John Wayne, Bette Davis, Lana Turner, Humphrey Bogart and Lauren Bacall — to name just a few!

Adding to the list of The Del's vacationing celebrities were stars who shot films at Naval Air Station North Island and stayed at the hotel. As the "Birthplace of Naval Aviation," North Island was an ideal location for Hollywood's popular aviation-themed movies, made all through the 1930s and 1940s. These included *Hell Divers* (1931) with Clark Gable and Wallace Beery; *Devil Dogs of the Air* (1935) with James Cagney and Pat O'Brien; *Wings Over Honolulu* (1937) with Ray Milland; *Wings of the Navy* (1939) with George Brent and Olivia de Havilland; *Flight Command* (1938) with Robert Taylor and Walter Pidgeon; and *Dive Bomber* (1941) with Errol Flynn, Fred MacMurray and Ralph Bellamy.

After World War II, television stars began to frequent the hotel, including Donna Reed, Carol Burnett, Raymond Burr, Doris Day, Dinah Shore, Dick Van Dyke and Walt Disney.

Privacy Please

Today's Hollywood celebrities still enjoy the Hotel del Coronado — although they do so privately. Gone are the days when a movie studio provided advance publicity and mandated professional photos poolside; today's actors like to enjoy their vacations unencumbered by fans or paparazzi.

Accordingly, the hotel staff handles celebrity arrangements discreetly, registering guests under pseudonyms, providing remote check-ins and making sure all aspects of their vacations are as private as possible. Beach Village — an exclusive enclave of luxury cottages right on the beach — has become a favored Del celebrity retreat, thanks to its private swimming pools, concierge services and ready access to the ocean.

FACING PAGE
Charlie Chaplin, shown here c. 1920, played polo while staying at The Del. Guest Emmie Spalding Hamilton recalled a vivid 1920s childhood memory of Chaplin, who walked by as her little sister, Eleanor, was rolling down a small grass embankment along the beach side of the hotel: "Two ladies and a man stopped and watched her, laughing and talking about the cute little blonde girl. The man was the famous comedian Charlie Chaplin, and I recognized him. He left the ladies and started rolling down the bank with Eleanor. She giggled, enjoying the silly man, but of course she had no idea who he was. The ladies were laughing, and I was spellbound. I remember wishing he would speak to me, too. After a while, Eleanor looked at him and waved her hand toward the 'audience' and said, 'Go back to those girls.' That 'brought down the house,' but I was humiliated."

Classic Celebrity Sightings

Lucille Ball and Desi Arnaz retreated to The Del for a lengthy stay in 1950 to fine-tune their "Ricky and Lucy" personas (which television executives had originally dismissed). After perfecting their routines in San Diego clubs, the duo signed a television contract and later featured The Del in a 1958 episode of *I Love Lucy*.

Errol Flynn was a frequent guest during the 1930s and 1940s, as one young visitor recalled: "Just before the war, I walked Errol Flynn's gorgeous Irish setter around the dock area and nearby for ten cents a walk." Apparently not everyone was as smitten with Flynn's pet; producer Hal Wallis remembered that the dog was ill-behaved, jumping up on hotel guests and even biting a waiter's leg.

Clark Gable, who stayed at The Del in 1931 during the filming of *Hell Divers*, enjoyed an ongoing relationship with the hotel. The *San Jose Mercury* reported in 1954: "Clark Gable always stops at Hotel del Coronado when he's on one of his La Paz fishing trips." A year later, Gable married actress Kay Williams, the former wife of Adolph Spreckels, son of hotel owner John D. Spreckels.

In 1947, a honeymoon couple caught a glimpse of the reclusive **Greta Garbo** (with a long cigarette holder) being ushered into a private dining room.

Piano maestro **Liberace** was playing to a less-than-sold-out audience when he was discovered at The Del in 1950. Fortunately, a television producer saw his show and immediately recognized the pianist's ability to connect to intimate groups, perfect for the "small screen."

A Navy wife during World War II recalls, "I remember one afternoon when **Robert Montgomery** walked through the lobby in his Navy uniform. He was very popular in those days and gorgeous."

One guest paid tribute to **Merle Oberon's** good looks (c. 1955), saying, "Her beauty was so much more off screen than on," and remembered the number of celebrities at the hotel: "A lot of stars came to Coronado at that time for a little bit of R&R, going without makeup, etc. so they wouldn't be recognized."

A c. 1939 newspaper article referenced a visit by **Mae West**, who "motored down for luncheon," after which she watched a badminton game in the Ballroom. When a young girl named May asked for her autograph, West wrote, "From Mae to May. Come up and see me sometime."

TOP
Lovely Lizabeth Scott posed in front of The Del in 1947.

THIS PAGE ABOVE
Clark Gable (right) with Wallace Beery and Cliff Edwards, who starred in Hell Divers *(1931), filmed on North Island.*

FACING PAGE
The Hotel del Coronado's wonderful collection of 1930s, '40s and '50s celebrity photos is a reflection of times gone by, when Hollywood studios expected their stars to share their private lives in public, and The Del employed a round-the-clock photographer. Shown here is just a small sampling (clockwise from top left): Errol Flynn (left) and friends enjoying a poolside cabana, c. 1939; Van Johnson between tennis games, c. 1945; Kirk Douglas mugging for the camera, with wife Dianne, c. 1950; Jane Russell with photographer, c. 1945; and George Sands (right) having cocktails, c. 1940. Many additional Hollywood couples are included in the hotel's book Celebrating Over a Century of Romance at the Hotel del Coronado: Engagements, Weddings, Honeymoons and Anniversaries.

Some Like It Hot!

Filmed at the Hotel del Coronado in 1958, *Some Like It Hot* showcased the talents of Marilyn Monroe, Tony Curtis and Jack Lemmon while also showing off the hotel's assets — a spectacular sun-drenched silhouette.

Named the number one comedy of all time by the American Film Institute, the movie has an honored place in film and Del history:

· Most of the cast and crew arrived in San Diego by train.

· Miami's mayor was miffed that The Del was chosen to represent a Florida resort. Coronado's mayor replied, "Some like it hot, but not as hot as Miami in September."

· Director Billy Wilder chose The Del for its vintage appeal (the story takes place during the 1920s), although at least one critic didn't believe the hotel was real, calling it "an uproariously improbable set."

· The movie lobby looks very similar to the hotel's lobby — but it's not; only exterior scenes were filmed at The Del (the movie lobby is also white).

· In the film, the hotel's original two front entrances are clearly visible (one was later removed).

· Marilyn Monroe's husband, esteemed playwright Arthur Miller, accompanied her to The Del.

· Tony Curtis was joined by his wife, actress Janet Leigh, who was pregnant with their daughter, Jamie Lee Curtis.

· One Coronado resident remembers Jack Lemmon water-skiing during his stay.

· It was reported that Monroe liked poached eggs in the morning and snacked on the hotel's vanilla soufflé.

· An 11-year-old boy was walking his Weimaraner at The Del one morning when he happened upon Monroe. After petting the dog, Monroe offered to give the boy a kiss. To his lifelong regret, he declined!

· Monroe — who could be a difficult performer — was at ease at The Del; Wilder thought that might have had something to do with the throng of her adoring fans.

· It was at The Del that Tony Curtis' character uttered the immortal line, "Some like it hot."

THIS PAGE ABOVE
Michael Margolin's family was arriving for their annual Del getaway just as Marilyn Monroe was being positioned for a scene. Margolin, who was 5 years old at the time, remembers being struck by the fact that his always-tennis-bound father put off his usual dash to the courts so he could take these photos of Monroe.

FACING PAGE
Marilyn Monroe charmed fans during the 1958 filming of Some Like It Hot.

THIS PAGE
Marilyn Monroe in her sequined dress (top left); Jack Lemmon chatting up his bandmates (top right); and Monroe and Curtis readying for a scene on Glorietta Bay (bottom left).

FACING PAGE
Off camera, Monroe and Jack Lemmon enjoyed a friendly relationship (top left); Tony Curtis standing as the "girls in the band" romp in the surf in the distance (right); and Monroe being instructed by director Billy Wilder (in shorts) as a Coronado policeman looks on (bottom left).

THIS PAGE TOP LEFT AND BOTTOM LEFT
The legacy of Some Like It Hot *lives on. In 1984, director Billy Wilder, along with Tony Curtis and Jack Lemmon, returned for a 25th anniversary celebration.*

THIS PAGE TOP RIGHT
An art contest held for the hotel's 120th birthday inspired this rendering of Tony Curtis and The Del by Silver Strand Elementary School student Isabel Salvatierra.

THIS PAGE BOTTOM RIGHT
In 2009, a Some Like It Hot *50th anniversary weekend featured a series of events, including an evening of reminiscences with Tony Curtis. Many fans arrived with their own memorabilia, such as this French* Some Like It Hot *movie poster, which a guest displayed in his window.*

FACING PAGE TOP LEFT AND BOTTOM LEFT
Director Billy Wilder was interviewed at The Del in 1984 (top). In 2012, Wilder was honored by the United States Postal Service in its film directors' series with a stamp that also included Monroe and the Hotel del Coronado.

FACING PAGE TOP RIGHT AND BOTTOM RIGHT
In 1995, the United States Postal Service unveiled the Marilyn Monroe stamp at the Hotel del Coronado.

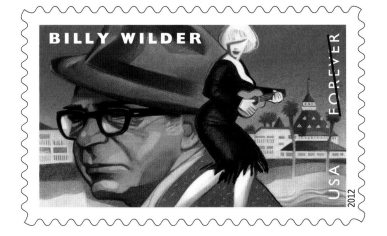

THIS PAGE
*Celebrity visitors from the 1960s and 1970s included
(clockwise from top left) Jerry Lewis, Lloyd Bridges,
Cary Grant and Frank Sinatra.*

THIS PAGE
The Stunt Man, *starring Peter O'Toole (bottom right), and filmed
at The Del in 1977–78, required the construction of a fake tower
atop the hotel's roof, followed by a dramatic explosion.*

Royal Visitors

King Kalakaua: The Hotel del Coronado received its first royal visitor when Hawaii's King Kalakaua came to call during his 1890 tour of California. Kalakaua was Hawaii's last king and the first ruling monarch to visit the United States. His trip began in San Francisco on December 4, 1890, where the citizenry celebrated with parades, banquets and balls. From there, King Kalakaua traveled south, stopping throughout California on his way to San Diego.

Kalakaua was a longtime friend of hotel owner John D. Spreckels, whose San Francisco–based father ("Sugar King" Claus Spreckels) owned sugar plantations in Hawaii. King Kalakaua stayed at the Hotel del Coronado for the length of his San Diego visit, arriving on December 28, 1890. The reigning royal was registered at The Del as "His Majesty King Kalakaua and Valet." Another four or five people (mostly with military titles) were checked in as part of his entourage. The group's collective residence was listed as San Francisco.

While at The Del, where Kalakaua reportedly retreated for health reasons, the king hosted events for San Diego's military officers, as well as for the people of Coronado. The visiting monarch, in turn, was honored at a steady stream of San Diego events, which overflowed with well-wishers.

Unfortunately, after leaving San Diego, King Kalakaua suffered a stroke in Santa Barbara, lapsing into a coma. Even so, the traveling group continued its trip back to San Francisco, where Kalakaua — with Claus Spreckels by his side — died on January 20, 1891. After his death, Kalakaua's sister, Lili'uokalani, became Hawaii's last monarch; her reign ended in January 1893.

Edward, Prince of Wales: Thirty years after Kalakaua's visit, another royal, England's Edward, Prince of Wales (later King Edward), was fêted at The Del. The reception and dinner on April 7, 1920 — attended by an estimated 1,000 guests — was held in the Crown Room and featured filet mignon and baked Alaska. Afterward, there was dancing in the Ballroom. The next day, a San Diego newspaper reported that The Del's celebration was "one of the most brilliant affairs in the history of the city ... the crowning event of a busy social season." That same day, the prince hosted a reception aboard the warship *Renown* for 400 invited guests.

An intriguing aspect of the prince's visit is the fact that his future wife was living in Coronado at the time. Wallis Warfield Spencer Simpson was a Coronado socialite then married to her first husband, Lieutenant Commander Earl Winfield Spencer, Jr. She would eventually divorce Spencer, marry her second husband, Ernest Simpson, move to England, befriend Prince Edward (who would ultimately become king), divorce her second husband and

wed Edward, who had to give up his throne to marry the twice-divorced American. After Edward's abdication and his marriage to Wallis, the couple became known as the Duke and Duchess of Windsor.

American Hero Charles Lindbergh

In 1927, famed aviator Charles Lindbergh was honored in the Crown Room after his successful transatlantic flight. His plane, *The Spirit of St. Louis*, had been built in San Diego, where Lindbergh oversaw its construction. After the plane was finished, Lindbergh flew from North Island to St. Louis (where his financial backers were) and then on to New York for the start of his flight.

At Lindbergh's Crown Room banquet on September 21, 1927, an estimated 1,000 guests enjoyed a decidedly Lindbergh-themed feast, which featured "Lone Eagle Stuffed Eggs," "Salad Lindbergh" and "Spirit of St. Louis Striped Bass."

Will Rogers, the era's universally loved actor, writer, humorist and world figure, was on hand to honor the aviator (Rogers' love of — and advocacy for — flying had earned him a friendship with Lindbergh). Typed on hotel stationery, Rogers' cryptic notes for the occasion indicate some of what he might have said during his speech, much of it paying homage to Lindbergh: "We thought of this country boy away out there on the ocean alone where no human being had ever been before ... we will never have a greater thrill during our lifetime." Rogers characterized Lindbergh's historic flight as "the most wished and prayed for event, after it started, that ever was ... prayed for in every known language."

Changing his tone, the humorist then pointed out that the 25-year-old pilot's record would no doubt be topped: "Engines will improve and things will get better, and your time will be beaten." But Rogers assured Lindbergh — who had munched on homemade sandwiches during the 33-hour flight across the ocean — that the pilot had "one record that I think will remain unsurpassed right on down through the ages ... [you'll always be remembered] as the only man who ever took a ham sandwich to Paris."

Continued on page 194

Men of Letters

L. Frank Baum: The author most associated with The Del is L. Frank Baum, who penned the *Wizard of Oz* series. Born in 1856, Baum adored the hotel, where he wintered regularly during the early 1900s. He called California the "Land of Enchantment ... where they grow sunshine and roses to offset our blizzards and icicles." Baum was so enamored of the hotel that he couldn't conceive of anyone not loving The Del, which he compared to heaven itself.

In a 1905 poem about Coronado ("scratched off," Baum said, in a half-hour while he and his wife were waiting for friends to join them for dinner in the Crown Room), he wrote, "And every day her loveliness shines pure, without a flaw; new charms entrance our every glance, and fill our souls with awe!" Not only was Baum fond of Coronado, Coronado was fond of Baum: In an article written about him for a San Diego student newspaper, the visiting author was described as "kind, genial, gentle-voiced, as true and fine a gentleman as I have ever met or expect to."

During his years in Coronado, Baum wrote four books in his Oz series: *Marvelous Land of Oz* (1904), *Dorothy and the Wizard of Oz* (1908), *The Road to Oz* (1909) and *The Emerald City of Oz* (1910). Although some conjecture that he based his design of Emerald City on the architecture of the Hotel del Coronado, Baum had already written about this fictitious setting in his first book, *The Wonderful Wizard of Oz*, before ever visiting the hotel.

Henry James: Henry James epitomized the well-to-do, socially prominent Victorian traveler. James was born in New York in 1843 and enjoyed a privileged upbringing that included intellectual pursuits and extensive world travel, later claiming Edith Wharton as one of his closest friends. James — who always preferred the sophisticated European to what he saw as the socially inept American — eventually settled in Europe and England full time.

In 1905, James went on an American speaking tour that took him from one coast to the other, bringing him to The Del, where he stayed from March 29 to April 6. In an April 5 letter, James wrote: "The days have been of heavenly beauty, and the flowers, the wild flowers just now in particular, which fairly *rage*, with radiance, over the land, are worthy of some purer planet than this. I live on oranges and olives, fresh from the tree, and I lie awake nights to listen, on purpose, to the languid lisp of the Pacific, which my windows overhang. It breaks my heart to have so stinted myself here — but it was inevitable, and no one had given me the least inkling that I should find California so sympathetic." In another letter, he referred to "the charming sweetness and comfort of this place."

THIS PAGE
The hotel honored Baum's legacy with an Oz-themed Christmas celebration in 1987 (top) and hosted some of the original movie Munchkins during The Del's centennial in 1988 (bottom).

FACING PAGE
A drawing of the Crown Room, c. 1915, featured the crown-shaped chandeliers said to have been designed by L. Frank Baum; a page from one of Baum's Oz series, The Emerald City of Oz, *referenced his 1910 Coronado writing location (bottom left); and a portrait of the author.*

PERHAPS I should admit on the title page that this book is "By L. Frank Baum and his correspondents," for I have used many suggestions conveyed to me in letters from children. Once on a time I really imagined myself "an author of fairy tales," but now I am merely an editor or private secretary for a host of youngsters whose ideas I am requested to weave into the thread of my stories.

These ideas are often clever. They are also logical and interesting. So I have used them whenever I could find an opportunity, and it is but just that I acknowledge my indebtedness to my little friends.

My, what imaginations these children have developed! Sometimes I am fairly astounded by their daring and genius. There will be no lack of fairy-tale authors in the future, I am sure. My readers have told me what to do with Dorothy, and Aunt Em and Uncle Henry, and I have obeyed their mandates. They have also given me a variety of subjects to write about in the future: enough, in fact, to keep me busy for some time. I am very proud of this alliance. Children love these stories because children have helped to create them. My readers know what they want and realize that I try to please them. The result is very satisfactory to the publishers, to me, and (I am quite sure) to the children.

I hope, my dears, it will be a long time before we are obliged to dissolve partnership.

Coronado, 1910   L. FRANK BAUM.

Other Authors: The Literary Del

Besides famed authors L. Frank Baum and Henry James, a number of other writers spent time at The Del, including:

Preeminent journalist **Joseph Pulitzer** visited in 1888. After being accosted in the lobby by an intrepid reporter, Pulitzer — who was called "the young Napoleon of journalism" — demanded, "How did you know I was here? I have hardly had time to know that I am here myself!"

William Gillette, who wrote the play *Sherlock Holmes* in 1898 while staying at The Del, performed in it on Broadway two years later.

Upton Sinclair, America's most famous muckraker, was "in residence" at The Del in 1916. Later he ran unsuccessfully for governor of California.

F. Scott Fitzgerald made a not-too-veiled reference to the hotel in *This Side of Paradise*, where he introduced character Amory

Blaine: "From his fourth to his tenth year, he *did* the country with his mother in her father's private car [including] Coronado, where his mother became so bored that she had a nervous breakdown in a fashionable hotel."

Edmund Wilson, journalist and close friend of Fitzgerald, wrote about The Del in 1931 for *The New Republic:* "It is the most magnificent example extant of the American seaside hotel … white and ornate as a wedding cake, polished and trim as a ship."

Legendary playwright **Arthur Miller** was at The Del during the filming of *Some Like It Hot*, and he frequently accompanied wife Marilyn Monroe to the set. Monroe — given to professional moodiness — was uncharacteristically carefree during her stay, but Miller was not; he was described by one reporter as a glum cigar-store Indian.

More-recent writers have included everyone from **Charles Schulz** to **Tennessee Williams** and **Truman Capote**. Perhaps no one was a more enthusiastic Del visitor than sci-fi writer **Ray Bradbury**, who said in a 1995 magazine article that he raised his daughters at the hotel, spending their summers in the sun for more than 30 years.

FACING PAGE
The Hotel del Coronado has attracted a range of luminaries, including this group of distinguished Americans (top): Harvey Firestone, Henry Ford, Thomas Edison and naturalist John Burroughs, c. 1915. In the 1920s, Babe Ruth enjoyed fishing at The Del (bottom left), while heavyweight champion Jack Dempsey took in Tent City (bottom right).

ABOVE LEFT
Arthur Miller and Marilyn Monroe in 1958.

ABOVE
San Diegan Theodor Geisel — America's Dr. Seuss — was a longtime fan of The Del and was photographed with wife Audrey at the hotel's 100th birthday celebration.

On the Guest Register — Historic Notables   **197**

In honour of

His Royal Highness, The Prince of Wales

Mayor and Mrs. Louis J. Wilde

Miss Lucile Wilde

will receive

on Wednesday evening the seventh of April

at ten o'clock

Hotel del Coronado

Dancing   *Admission
                        by card enclosed*

THIS PAGE

Clockwise from top left: After arriving via a British warship, Edward, Prince of Wales, was transferred to a skiff for the ride to the hotel; with San Diego Mayor Louis J. Wilde, who hosted the prince's party in conjunction with his daughter's debutante ball; the 1920 dinner invitation for the Crown Room included dancing afterward in the Ballroom.

FACING PAGE

Clockwise from top: The Crown Room head table (Prince Edward is in the center of the photo, with his head bowed in conversation); a handwritten welcome note from Coronado's British contingent; and Coronado socialite Wallis Simpson, whom Edward would woo and wed in the 1930s.

To H.R.H. The Prince of Wales.

These flowers are but a small token of admiration and respect felt for you by a group of British-born women of Coronada. They see in your devotion to duty; your courage on the Field of Battle; your service for others; so cheerfully and charmingly given, the promise that even when your glorious youth is over, the God given gifts you possess will be placed at the service of not only our own Mighty Empire but to that of Humanity at Large.

FOLLOWING PAGE
Charles Lindbergh's 1927 banquet in the Crown Room; inset, the pilot with The Spirit of St. Louis.

CITIZENS BANQUET TO COLONEL CHARLES A. LINDBERG.
AUSPICES SAN DIEGO CHAMBER of COMMERCE.
HOTEL DEL CORONADO, SEPT 21-1927.

On the Guest Register — Historic Notables

The Ghost of Kate Morgan

The Beautiful Stranger

Kate Morgan was a pretty woman in her mid-20s who checked into the Hotel del Coronado on Thursday, November 24, 1892, registering under the name "Lottie A. Bernard" from Detroit. Five days later, her lifeless body was found on an exterior staircase leading to the beach, with a gunshot wound to her head, which the San Diego coroner later determined was self-inflicted.

Because the police found nothing to positively identify Kate as Lottie, a description of Kate and the circumstances of her death were telegraphed to police agencies around the country, after which the press began to refer to Kate as the "Beautiful Stranger." Eventually, an unknown source identified "Lottie" as Kate Morgan, originally from Iowa, the granddaughter of Joe W. Chandler, who resided in Riverton, Iowa.

Once it was revealed that Kate had used an alias, speculation soon followed. Adding to the conjecture was the fact she had been traveling alone, something women generally did not do in 1892, and that she had arrived without luggage. Kate was also reported to be sickly — complaining of stomach cancer — and despondent, always on the lookout for a "brother" who was supposed to join her at The Del. No one ever showed up, and after Kate took her own life, it was speculated by some that she had been deserted by a lover.

Kate's story was both heart-wrenching and tantalizing, and details were widely reported in newspapers throughout California, with the tone of the articles varying between compassionate concern and sordid speculation. San Diego's *Seaport News* portrayed Kate in a December 3 article as a tragic figure, filled with grief and pain:

> She was reserved and mingling not with the other guests, made few acquaintances. It was known, however, that she was an invalid. On Monday, she resolved to end her sorrows and sufferings. Soon after dark on that evening, she deserted the warm cheerful rooms of the hotel for the darkness outside, and on the steps at the rear, in the cold, drizzling rain, took her own life.

Another article in the *San Diego Union*, published two days before the *Seaport News* article, took a decidedly different point of view:

> For every fact brought out in the investigation of the suicide of the pretty and mysterious stranger at Hotel del Coronado tending to show that the act was done in despondency over sickness, there are dozens of circumstances pointing strongly to the theory that she was betrayed, ruined and deserted, and committed the act soon after the truth dawned on her.

Resident Ghost

All these years later, it's impossible to know for sure what Kate's life was like or why it ended. But it is believed by some that the spirit of Kate Morgan still resides at The Del, where paranormal activity has often been reported by guests and employees. The incidents are generally benign in nature, many having to do with electrical oddities (a television set mysteriously turns itself on), inexplicable sounds or fragrances.

The room in which Kate stayed, numbered 302 at that time, reports its own share of activity - and is the most requested guestroom in the hotel. Her ghostly figure is also often witnessed near the beach.

Another very "active" area is the resort's gift shop, Est. 1888, where employees routinely witness giftware mysteriously flying off shelves, oftentimes falling upright and always unbroken. Some paranormal researchers believe that Kate likes to frequent Est. 1888 because its vintage-inspired hotel memorabilia feels familiar to her. But shop employees have another theory: Because memorabilia related to Marilyn Monroe's 1958 hotel filming of *Some Like It Hot* seems to be the most prone to tumbling, they speculate that The Del's resident ghost doesn't like sharing the spotlight with the Hollywood star.

FACING PAGE
Reenactment photos of Kate's visit — using a model in period costume — were created to illustrate the resort's book Beautiful Stranger: The Ghost of Kate Morgan and the Hotel del Coronado.

HOTEL DEL CORONADO,

E. S. BABCOCK, Manager.   Coronado, California.

Money, Jewels, and other valuable Packages, must be placed in the Safe in the office, otherwise the Proprietors will not be responsible for any loss.

NAMES.	RESIDENCE.	ROOMS.	TIME.
Thursday Nov. 24th 1892			
Mark T. Williams	N.Y. City	300	L.
Henry Pereira	Pawtucket R.I.	152	"
Mr. R.H. Gage	Pawtucket R.I.	153	"
Mrs M.E. French	Pawtucket R.I.	153	"
Geo Neate	Detroit Mich	113	"
Mrs R. Irwin	Denver Colo	315	"
Grace Irwin	Denver Colo	315	"
Miss Lottie A Bernard	Detroit	302	b
Jos A Jones	Boston	371	"
Ira Clark + wife	Coroner	died	"
Fran E Clark	"		"
H.C. Moore	New Mex	196	S.

CERTIFICATE OF DEATH. ✓ 188

CORONER'S OFFICE,
CITY AND COUNTY OF SAN DIEGO.

San Diego, Cal., Dec 12 1892.

Name Mrs Kate Morgan

Aged 24 years,   Male. Female.

Occupation ———— Married. Single. Widow. Widower.

Place of Birth State or Country Iowa   Nationality American

How long resident of this City or County, 4 days years.

Previous Residence, Los Angeles   Race White

Place of Death, Corona do Beach,

Date of Death, November 29 1892

Date of Burial, December 13th 1892

Place of Interment, Mt Hope Cemetery.

Johnson & Co Undertaker.

CORONER'S CERTIFICATE.

I, M.B. Kellar, Coroner, do hereby Certify, that having made all needed examination and inquiries on the body of above described decedent, I do hereby certify, that Mrs Kate came to her death in this County by a pistol shot inflicted by her own hand with suicidal intent

M.B. Kellar.
Coroner, City and County San Diego.
By H. Stetson Deputy Coroner

THIS PAGE TOP LEFT
The name "Miss Lottie A. Bernard" was entered in the guest register on Thursday, November 24, 1892 (it is the eighth entry). However, the desk clerk signed for Kate; it is not her handwriting.

THIS PAGE BOTTOM LEFT
Based on the coroner's inquest, Kate's death was ruled a suicide, although by today's standards, the investigation was rushed (conducted the day after the body was found) and perfunctory, with inconclusive results.

THIS PAGE TOP RIGHT
After Kate Morgan's grandfather, J.W. Chandler, was located in Iowa, he was contacted regarding her death, to which he replied with a short telegram: "Bury her and send me statement." Kate's public funeral was held at the undertaker's two weeks after she died, by which time Kate's sad passing had captured the hearts of many San Diegans. As a result, a proper service was held, with a reverend officiating and the brotherhood of St. Andrew in attendance. According to a San Diego Union article on December 14, 1892, "Quite a number of persons were present. At the close of the service, the casket was placed in the hearse for conveyance to Mount Hope Cemetery, where the body was interred."

FACING PAGE
A reenactment photo captures a likeness of Kate Morgan.

FOLLOWING PAGE
"Kate" at The Del.

TAKING LIFE EASY — HOTEL CORONADA